LETTERS OF ENCOURAGEMENT

A CURATED COLLECTION OF ESSAYS FROM **HIGHER THINGS**

Published by:
1517 Publishing
PO Box 54032
Irvine, CA 92619-4032

Publisher's Cataloging-In-Publication Data
(Prepared by The Donohue Group, Inc.)

Names: Higher Things (Organization), editor.
Title: Letters of encouragement : a curated collection of essays from Higher
    Things / [edited by] Higher Things
Description: Irvine, CA : Higher Things, an imprint of New Reformation
    Publications, [2023] | Includes bibliographical references.
Identifiers: ISBN: 978-1-956658-32-3 (paperback) | 978-1-956658-33-0 (ebook)
Subjects: LCSH: Lutheran Church—Clergy—Correspondence. |
    Lutheran Church—Clergy. | Christian leadership. | Pastoral theology. |
    Encouragement—Religious aspects—Christianity. | LCGFT: Essays. |
    BISAC: RELIGION / Christian Ministry / Pastoral Resources. | RELIGION /
    Christian Ministry / General. | RELIGION / Christianity / Lutheran.
Classification: LCC: BX8071 .L48 2023 | DDC: 284.1—dc23

Printed in the United States of America.

Cover art by Ronda Palazzari.

LETTERS OF ENCOURAGEMENT

A CURATED COLLECTION OF ESSAYS FROM **HIGHER THINGS**

Table of contents

Contributors

Rev. Timothy Appel is the pastor at Grace Lutheran Church in Smithville, Texas. He is also the host of *Sharper Iron*, a Bible study radio program and podcast on KFUO.

Rev. Roy S. Askins is a husband of one and father of seven. Currently, he serves as the managing editor of *The Lutheran Witness*, the flagship periodical of The Lutheran Church—Missouri Synod. Prior to this work, he served as a missionary in the Asia region and a pastor in east Texas.

Rev. Duane Bamsch is the pastor at Grace Lutheran Church in Grass Valley, California and the president of Higher Things.

Rev. Seth Clemmer is the senior pastor at Bethany Lutheran Church and School in Naperville, Illinois.

Rev. Sean Daenzer is LCMS director of worship and chaplain at the International Center. He lives in southern Illinois with his wife Audrey and four daughters. He formerly served as pastor of a dual parish in southeast North Dakota.

Rev. Michael Daniels is pastor at Redeemer Lutheran Church in Catawba, North Carolina. He is husband to Emily and dad to Lillian, Rebekah, and Enoch.

Rev. Aaron T. Fenker is the pastor of Bethlehem and Immanuel Lutheran churches in Bremen, Kansas. He also served as the dean of theology for Higher Things.

Rev. Harrison Goodman is the content executive for Higher Things.

Rev. Dr. Matthew C. Harrison is the president of the Lutheran Church–Missouri Synod.

Rev. Dr. Erik Herrmann is professor of Historical Theology, dean of Theological Research and publication, and director of the Center for Reformation Research at Concordia Seminary, St. Louis, Missouri.

Rev. Chris Hull is the husband of Allison Monk Hull, and Dad to Lochlann, Eamonn, Tiernann, Jameson, Avonlea, and Killiann Hull. He is the pastor of Zion Lutheran Church in Tomball, Texas. He co-hosts with Patrick Sturdivant *There and Back Again,* a Higher Things Podcast.

Rev. Kyle Krueger is the associate pastor at Glory of Christ Lutheran Church in Plymouth, Minnesota.

Rev. Dr. James Ambrose Lee II is associate professor of theology at Concordia University Chicago, where he is the chair of the Division of Theology and the director of the Honors Program. Dr. Lee studies nineteenth-century German theology. He and his wife, Emily, have been (thus-far) blessed with two children, Ambrose and Cecilia.

Rev. Christopher Neuendorf serves as pastor at the tri-point parish of Our Savior's Bottineau, St. Paul Rugby, and Immanuel Willow Creek, North Dakota. He and his wife Leah have been blessed so far with two precious children who love the Lord their God.

Rev. Anthony Oliphant serves as pastor at Redeemer Lutheran Church in Elmhurst, Illinois. He is also an adjunct theology professor at Concordia University-Chicago and works with the St. Philip Lutheran Mission Society to train future pastors in Africa.

Rev. Dr. Roger C. Paavola served congregations in Manitoba, Canada and Cookeville, Tennessee before becoming the LCMS Mid-South District President in 2012.

Rev. Dr. John T. Pless has served on the faculty of Concordia Theological Seminary in Fort Wayne, Indiana since 2000. From 1983-2000, he was campus pastor at University Lutheran Chapel in Minneapolis. He is also the author or editor of numerous books including *Pastor Craft* and *Luther's Small Catechism: A Manual for Discipleship.*

Rev. Dr. Matthew R. Richard is the pastor at St. Paul's Lutheran Church in Minot, North Dakota.

Rev. Gary W. Schultz is the kantor at Immanuel Evangelical Lutheran Church in Terre Haute, Indiana.

Rev. Dr. Gregory P. Seltz is the executive director at the Lutheran Center for Religious Liberty in Washington D.C.

Rev. Dr. Scott Stiegemeyer is the associate professor of Theology and Bioethics and director of Pre-Seminary and Pre-Deaconess Programs Concordia University-Irvine, California.

Rev. Ralph Tausz is the pastor of The Evangelical Lutheran Church of the Apostles in Melrose Park, Illinois. He and his wife Amy have been blessed with five children.

Rev. David Vandercook lives in Arkansas with his wife, Laura, and three children, Allyssa, David, and Kaytlin. He serves Shepherd of Peace Lutheran Church in Maumelle and Trinity Lutheran Church in North Little Rock.

Rev. Bryan Wolfmueller is the pastor of St. Paul and Jesus Deaf Lutheran Churches in Austin, Texas. He is the author of *Take They Our Life: Martin Luther's Theology of Martyrdom, A Martyr's Faith for a Faithless World, Has American Christianity Failed?* and *Final Victory: Contemplating the Death and Funeral of a Christian.* He is host of *What-Not: The Podcast,* and the co-host of *Table Talk Radio* podcast, and is involved in numerous other theological projects. He and his wife Keri live with their four children in Round Rock, Texas.

Rev. Andrew T. Yeager is the pastor of St. Paul Lutheran Church in Decatur, Indiana.

Introduction

Rev. Dr. Matthew C. Harrison

It must have been about 1974, prior to my confirmation. A young assistant pastor came to our church. He carried himself well. He had a great sense of humor. He was engaged with the youth of the congregation, and he had a cool car. He had come to visit me at home after I'd been in a serious moto-cross motorcycle accident which could easily have taken my life but left me with 60 stitches in my face. No other pastor had ever come to our home. I volunteered as a 7th grader to assist with VBS because that young pastor (later to become my brother-in-law) caused me to think for the first time in my life that I might just like to become a pastor, too.

That's what the studies tell us. Most decide or have an inkling of becoming a pastor at about the 7th grade. (To be sure, there are many different experiences!) I trusted in Jesus completely, though I was no young Lutheran genius, that's for sure. I was studying the *Small Catechism* in confirmation and memorizing both the catechism and key verses from the explanation. "With food and raiment let us be therewith content!" That's one that was seared forever into my mind, and precisely *because* the King James was so unfamiliar! My family were LCMS Christians. My parents made sure we were in church, Sunday school, and "mid-week" for confirmation studies. My dad insisted on getting to "early church," and we had no choice! "UP and at 'em boys!" he'd holler into our bedroom. I would not have been hooked into considering the pastorate by my future brother-in-law, had my parents not set the stage, and had in the position where I needed to be to be influenced.

I don't think I told anyone I wanted to be a pastor. And that desire faded and waned, then came to the fore again. My parents hadn't been encouraging me in that direction, not because they at all disrespected the profession or their pastors (quite the opposite as I never recall either of them making fun of or dissing one of our pastors). I think it was just kind of "outside their wheelhouse." It hadn't been part of their long-term family experience as Lutheran Christians.

High school brought a lot of growth. Unfortunately, I went in the direction of the Fellowship of Christian Athletes for a time (still attending my LCMS church). Well meaning, but misled individuals had us constantly "taking our spiritual temperature," asking what "quarter" we were in in our walk with Christ. "Fourth quarter" was the goal of spiritual endeavors. This brand of popular evangelical pietism had me constantly looking at myself instead of Jesus. And I was quite convinced I was something! The leadership was focused on directing me away from trust in Holy Baptism (the forgiveness of sins! Titus 3), trust in Absolution (forgiveness, John 20:23f), and Lord's Supper (the forgiveness of sins! "Given and shed for you for the forgiveness of sins.") And worst of all, I was constantly being pushed to "decide for Christ," and being told by "counselors," openly or not so openly, that being Lutheran was a problem.

God was merciful. Of all the passages I memorized (and too often barely memorized or not at all) for catechism class, the meaning of the Second Article of the Apostles' Creed stuck with me, hard. "I believe that I cannot believe in Jesus Christ my Lord or come to Him, but that He has called me by the Gospel…" I had bought into evangelical Christianity, giving "testimonials" wherever I could, about how I had made the right decision to follow Christ completely, and that my life (nearly sin-free) was a glowing example of the great things that could happen to others if they just made the same wise choice to put Jesus first in their lives.

Somehow, I did not follow through and leave my Lutheran congregation as other friends had. I realized this approach to Christianity was complete nonsense. I knew the Law and I knew full well that I—precisely as a Christian—did not, could not, live up to the demands of the Law. I was a sinner. I read Paul in Romans 7 and it resonated completely with me. "The good that I want to do, I do not do. But the evil that I do not want, this I do . . . O wretched man that I am!"

Through college I'd been taking religious studies courses. I came to realize that while I was no evangelical, neither was I a protestant liberal. At that time the emphasis where I was studying was on religious pluralism, the universality of salvation no matter what religion, situational ethics, no sure moral norms outside the self, and very little concern for what the New Testament or creedal Christianity has taught for millennia. Somehow by sheer grace, the God of all mercy in Jesus sustained me, even if in my spiritual growth I had come merely to realize what I was *not*, more than realizing what I was as a confessional Lutheran. The draw to become a pastor persisted.

A new vicar (a second-career guy out of the Ft. Wayne seminary) arrived at our congregation. He played a very cool, old Gibson flat top guitar. I liked that guitar. I played guitar and banjo, or at least tried. I liked our vicar. He was a lovely man; still is. The woman who would become my wonderful wife of 40 years was already by my side. I wanted to go to the Ft. Wayne seminary like that vicar. She was completely supportive, set high standards for love and honor, and with love and forgiveness, began to make me far more than I could have been without her. Last summer on vacation my two sons began asking me if they could help me "do this," "carry that," etc. My first thought was, "What do these kids want from me now?" I soon realized that their wives had directed them to look after their dad. Just like Kathy for me, so my daughters-in-law are making better men out of my sons.

I showed up at Concordia Seward for the spring semester of 1984. I desperately wanted some prep for the seminary. I began studying C.F.W. Walther's *Law and Gospel* (a classic every pastor must read, and every layperson should read), and *A Theology to Live By: The Practical Luther for the Practicing Christian,* by Herman A. Preus. I was home. Studying at seminary blew our minds. I say "our" because Kathy and I had married at 21 and 19, so we grew theologically together at the sem. I had gotten a fantastic grounding in New Testament Greek at Seward and studying the text of the Bible and all the great verses on Baptism, Word of God, Absolution, Lord's Supper, eternal election, grace, faith, etc., lit a fire in my gut for the precious Bible. Studying Lutheran theology and the *Lutheran*

Confessions fanned the flame. They are directed completely toward pastoral concerns, including assurance, certainty of salvation, clear faith in Christ and His Cross alone. The furnace was lit; it rages and roars with a flame inextinguishable to this moment.

Serving as a pastor is an amazing job. You're expected to read the Bible! You're expected to preach and teach the Bible! What you teach you must learn! You're expected to have your Bible open on your desk for study! You preach sermons on Sunday to people whom you actually come to know Monday through Saturday! Visiting homes and businesses gives you an insight into the lives of people, with all their blessings and challenges (and they've got 'em all!). After all these years, nothing surprises me. But when something is confessed, the pastor's ears are a tomb. What goes in, never (and I mean *never*) comes out. Visiting teaches you what in the lives of people you need to preach to, what they need to hear in terms of crushing Law and sweetest Gospel. Preaching is not easy, but a pastor works on it, and gets better over time, coming to know both text and people better and better. And, like Luther wrote once, "It's suffering that brings it all together." The pastor will suffer crosses. But God's richest blessings come in the form of the Cross (Romans 5-8). I often say a pastor truly is not worth his salt until a congregation's voters' assembly has handed him his rear end a few times. *(Smile)*

Being a pastor is the greatest possible honor. It's amazing that people invite you into their lives at their absolute worst, most painful, and even embarrassing moments, when they desperately need the Word of God and forgiveness and hope. And they invite a pastor into their best moments, like Baptisms, confirmations, graduations, marriages, and anniversaries. What a privilege to be at the bedside when a saint dies, to learn how to speak the Word of God for comfort, to sing Easter hymns to the dying only to have the family ask, "Pastor, can we sing that one you sang with Mom in the hospital, 'I Know That My Redeemer Lives?'" Sure thing.

It's not easy business. Never has been. Just read the Gospels, Acts, and Paul's letters. There are crosses aplenty. Read the biographies of Luther or Dr. Walther, or F.C.D. Wyneken. Brilliant pastors all, who suffered their own personal weakness, and those of others. But that's the way of the Great Shepherd of the Sheep, the great Pastor, Jesus. To serve is to take on the weaknesses of those served, just like Jesus took on the weaknesses and frail flesh of mankind in order to save us all. Over time, a pastor learns to say with John the Baptizer, "I must decrease, and [Jesus] must increase."

Consider being a pastor. Your sins are forgiven in Christ. You are certainly free to serve in any God-pleasing vocation. God needs lawyers and farmers and doctors and teachers. If you're meant to be a pastor, the Church will push you along at key moments. Many will come along the way to help financially and otherwise. Your teachers will encourage you and help you discern the path forward. Ultimately, Christ will work His sure will through a divine call to a congregation, for you to "preach and teach." It's a humbling thing to be the mouth of God Himself when speaking the clear Word of God in the Absolution. "In the stead and by the command of Christ, I forgive you." It's a humbling thing to be the very hands of Jesus baptizing a baby. It's a very humbling thing to learn to serve as Jesus serves, "having this mind in you that was in Christ ... serving unto death, even death on a cross."

A lot of young people these days are preoccupied with money. It's never been different really. If you don't become a pastor, go earn a lot of money and be generous to your family and your church. If you become a pastor, the Lord will provide, and indeed, more remarkably than you can imagine (2 Corinthians 8:1-7).

Letter 1 - Pastor as Vocation

Rev. Andrew T. Yeager

We Lutherans frequently refer to the term "vocation" which means calling, or station in life. In the way that we use the word in the Church, a vocation is more than a job. Jobs are given by people. Vocations are given by God.

Vocations are stations. Think of a Roman soldier, stationed at a particular spot along a border wall to stand sentinel through the watches of night (Mark 6:30-44; John 6:1-15). No other soldier has been commanded to stand there, in that one precise place in the line, but that one soldier alone. That is vocation. So, what is yours?

Go to Section 3 in your *Small Catechism*, the "Table of Duties." Listed there are the titles of several vocations. Some of these describe you. There is the vocation of hearer of God's Word, that is, a Christian. God called you to that one in your Baptism. He called you to be a member of the Holy Christian Church and a member of a local congregation. You will stand in that vocation your whole life.

Through marriage, there is the vocation of husband and wife. And from marriage comes the vocation of father and mother. Being a child is a vocation, too. There is the vocation of citizen of your country. There are the vocations of government offices, employers, workers, youth, widows. And there is the vocation of pastor. You can see how some vocations have been given to you, but not all.

Why does God call us to vocations? Because He wants us in a suitable space where we can love and serve our neighbor. And yes, everyone is a neighbor (Luke 10:25-37). But your vocation puts certain neighbors before you in a unique way and makes you certain they are your neighbors whom God is calling you to love.

God makes two things clear: what your vocation is, and who the neighbors are. A husband's wedding band is a sure sign to him that he is in fact a husband and points to the woman he married—not to any girl, but to the one who put that ring on his finger on their wedding day. Children playing with their friends outside don't run to just any house when the dinner bell rings; they know which table in what house will have food and the parents who prepared it waiting for them. The IRS leaves no room for doubt as to which national treasury your tax check is going to supply. So, Christians know their vocations, and they know the neighbors whom their vocations bind them to.

This, too, is true of pastors. I am a pastor. God has left no room for doubt about that. And, He has left no room for doubt about whom I am to serve. I am not called to just a random congregation in Dublin or Denver or Dubai, but rather to that one congregation on the outskirts of Decatur, Indiana, where He placed me.

My first call out of seminary was to be an admissions counselor. I recruited future pastors for one of our synod's seminaries for three years. I talked with men who were aspiring to the vocation of pastor. Sometimes, prospective students would say things like, "I think God is calling me to be a pastor." I would often sense a hint of reluctance or unease there. As in, "I think this could be the case … but I am not really sure." It is at that point I would remind them that, in fact, God definitely had not called them to be pastor yet. But with God's help and after years of preparation at the seminary, He might.

Here's the thing about God's call to be a pastor: He doesn't leave it a mystery. When He calls you, you know. You know because the call doesn't come immediately, that is, without human agents. God doesn't lay the call on your heart, so that you must perceive it through feelings or intuitions. Sometimes in the Old Testament, God called men immediately, as He did the prophet Samuel (1 Samuel 3). But now, the regular way God calls men into the Office of the Holy Ministry is externally, through His Church.

In my study, I have hanging on my wall a "Diploma of Vocation." My church sent it to me in the mail after they called me to be their pastor in 2018. I look at it occasionally, just as I often look down at the wedding ring on my left ring finger. This document, like my wedding ring, signifies what God has made me by His call. I am a pastor. God doesn't ever want me to doubt or second guess that.

God is all about certainty. God joins His Holy Word to water, bread, wine, and the voice of your pastor so that you—baptized, absolved, and fed the Body and Blood of Jesus—might have certainty that God has forgiven your sins. Likewise, God makes His call into the ministry certain because He wants the men whom He calls to be certain that their place is God's place for them. He wants them to perform their duties with a boldness that arises from the foundation of God's sure and certain Word.

If I was unsure of whether I was called by God to be a pastor—if God left this up to chance, or the subjective feelings of my heart— then what would happen when Satan turns up the fire on me? When the world pushes back against my confession and faith? Or when people refuse to hear and listen to me? Or, worst of all, when I sin and fall short of this high and holy calling (which I do, daily and much)?

If the call to be a pastor came only from men and not from God, or, if God left the perception of His call up to my own subjective feelings—"I feel called to be a pastor"—then the moment resistance came, it would be easy to lose heart. I might start thinking, "Maybe the people who called me didn't know what they were doing," or, "Maybe the feelings I had years ago were wrong." At that point, I might want to jump ship and leave the ministry altogether. But—and God be praised for this—God hasn't founded His call on shifting sand. We pastors have this ministry, this Office, this vocation as a certain call from God.

It should also be said that the call gives the pastor's congregation certainty, too. At times, churches might get fed up with their shepherd—and sometimes, for good reason. Their pastor is a sinner just like they are. The call from God reminds the church that this man really is God's man for them, their own shepherd.

And, the call isn't founded upon our merit or worthiness, either. Every pastor stands before the immense task lying before him, owning his own unworthiness, and his inability to carry it out. In this, pastors are like the twelve disciples right before Jesus fed the five thousand. Jesus says, "You give them something to eat!" The disciples protest and say that 200 denarii-worth of bread won't make a dent in the hunger of that enormous crowd. "We have five loaves and two fish, but what are they among so many?" (Mark 6:30-44; John 6:1-15) What they were saying to Jesus was, "Lord, we don't have the resources within ourselves to do what you have called us to do."

Every pastor can say the same thing. There is no way we can care for the people of God out of our own stock and store. We don't have what it takes. We are not good enough, faithful enough, smart enough. Of ourselves, we simply are not up to the job (I mean, vocation).

But, as Paul says, we have "this ministry by the mercy of God" (2 Corinthians 4:1). Pastors serve in a high and holy vocation. But they are sinners, too. And yet, Jesus Christ forgives their sins through Word and Sacrament. It is this very forgiveness that pastors are not only to hand over to God's people. It is this very forgiveness that pastors are called to trust and rely upon for their own life and salvation. Christ makes men faithful pastors by His Word of forgiveness. It is already on account of God's mercy that we are Christians. Baptism is mercy. Absolution and the Lord's Supper are mercy. And it is by God's mercy that pastors are called to their vocation, unworthy though they are to fill it out by their own reason and strength.

The desire to become a pastor is a godly aspiration. The Holy Spirit cultivates this desire in the hearts of men who hear the Word. So, if you are thinking of becoming a pastor, give your pastor a call today. There is no person better suited to guide you and help you discern than the man who once sought the Holy Office himself and wrestled with the same questions any prospective student of the seminary does.

Letter 2 - Pastor as Preacher

Rev. Ralph Tausz

A preacher must be both soldier and shepherd. He must nourish, defend and teach; he must have teeth in his mouth, and be able to bite and fight.

~ *Dr. Martin Luther*

When a group of Lutherans in early America chose the green rolling hills of Gettysburg, Pennsylvania as the site for their seminary, who would have ever thought that it would one day be the location of the bloodiest battle ever fought on American soil? The beaches and chalk-white cliffs of Normandy, France are breathtaking in beauty. Who would have ever thought that they would one day be a battlefield soaked with the crimson blood of thousands who gave their lives for their country on D-Day?

Similarly, when God was shaping the soil of Eden into an ear and affixing it to the head of the first man, who would have ever thought that God was placing onto this wondrous creation, what would become the bloodiest of battlefields, where the casualty count would be the entire human race?

The forces of evil did, led by a preacher named Satan. Satan is a preacher, and he fights with his mouth. He preaches God's Word, but with his own deadly spin. God created the ear as the organ of faith. The ear was to take in God's Word and cherish it, but our first parents gave ear to the wrong preacher, and this brought sin, death, and eternal damnation to all of mankind.

But God is a God who also fights with His mouth. He preached into those fallen ears of Adam and Eve the promise of a Preacher to come, Jesus Christ, God in the flesh (Genesis 3:15). And, oh, what glorious Good News came from between those teeth!

Jesus came preaching. He was committed to preaching. His love for mankind compelled Him to preach. "I must preach the good news of the Kingdom of God … for I was sent for this purpose" (Luke 4:43). But preaching is never a leisurely task. It's always a battle with Satan and his minions who don't want Christ's Gospel in human ears. Jesus' first sermon in His hometown of Nazareth almost got Him thrown off a cliff. Jesus preached, and the proud scoffed. Jesus preached, and demons were driven away. Jesus preached, and it unplugged the ears of a deaf man and unchained his tongue. Jesus preached, but only the poor in spirit heard Him gladly. His opponents could only muzzle this Preacher by putting Him to death on a cross, but He even turned that into a pulpit, where He preached a brief but marvelous sermon as He was offering Himself as the all-sufficient sacrifice for the atonement of all sinners: "It is finished." Indeed, here was the Good Shepherd, laying down His life for the sheep. But here was also our Good Soldier, the Captain of our Salvation, suffering unspeakable hardship to redeem sinners.

But Jesus was not done preaching, for He was "delivered up for our trespasses and raised for our justification" (Romans 4:25). Raised on the Third Day, He opened His mouth and preached some more. On the eve of that day, He preached the peace of His forgiveness into the ears of His first pastors, those scared disciples hiding behind locked doors. He then preached some more to them that evening and established the Preaching Office, so "that repentance and forgiveness of sins should be proclaimed in his name to all nations, beginning in Jerusalem" (Luke 24:46-47).

"The saying is trustworthy: If anyone aspires to the office of overseer, he desires a noble task" (1 Timothy 3:1). An overseer is a pastor. The word "pastor" comes from the Latin word for "shepherd." A pastor has many noble duties. He administers the Sacraments. He prays for the flock. He labors in Word and doctrine so that he can instruct both young and old. He forgives the sins of the penitent, promising never to divulge those sins. He cares for the poor and visits the sick and dying. He aims to be a godly example to the flock. And yet, his noblest duty is to fight with His mouth. His most important duty is to preach. That's why our *Lutheran Confessions* call the Office of the Holy Ministry, "the Preaching Office." It is so important, in fact, that the Lord says to those in that office: "The one who hears you, hears me" (Luke 10:16).

"So faith comes from hearing, and hearing through the word of Christ" (Romans 10:17). The human ear is still a battlefield. Thankfully, the Lord still graciously gifts His Church with preachers so that the ears of sinners might take in the Gospel, have faith in Jesus, and be justified. Preachers are God's fighters on the frontline. They are called to proclaim God's Word, not their own. They are called to teach God's pure doctrine, not their own opinions. They are to be outfitted with the best weaponry, which is not human eloquence, but God's Holy Word, which is "living and active, sharper than any two-edged sword" (Hebrews 4:12). God's Word alone is the weapon that has the power to make Satan and his forces retreat. "For the weapons of our warfare are not of the flesh but have divine power to destroy strongholds" (2 Corinthians 10:4).

God promises that His Word preached always accomplishes what He pleases. Still, preachers are tempted to lose heart. It often seems like it's not accomplishing anything. Satan has blinded the minds of unbelievers, and he's busy snatching the Word from their ears. The ears of the faithful can become bored with God's Word and itch for other "gospels." Ears become stubborn and harden, so God's Word bounces off them. The Word of God is always a confrontation with the flesh and that's not always so well received. All the while Satan continues to send false preachers proclaiming a false Jesus. Even Dr. Luther struggled with the task. He became so frustrated with the stubborn ears of the Wittenberg faithful that he refused to preach for nine months. He who so highly extolled the Preaching Office even once said, "I would rather be stretched on a wheel or carry stones than preach one sermon" (Fred Meuser, *Luther the Preacher*. Minneapolis: Augsburg Publishing House 1983, p. 276-277).

But the preacher need not lose heart. The Lord of the Church who calls and ordains men to this task, has his back. "Therefore, having this ministry by the mercy of God, we do not lose heart" (2 Corinthians 4:1). It's because of God's mercy that preachers are called and ordained into the Preaching Office. The preacher need not lose heart because it was mercy that placed him into that high office and it is mercy that will sustain him as he carries out this noblest of tasks. Furthermore, the Lord does not require certain results, success, or human applause. Thankfully, even the competence to carry out the work is from God. "Such is the confidence that we have through Christ toward God. Not that we are sufficient in ourselves to claim anything as coming from us, but our sufficiency is from God" (2 Corinthians 3:4-5). The attitude of preachers can be that of another preacher, John the Baptist: "He must increase, but I must decrease" (John 3:30). Or, as one of our faithful Lutheran fathers once put it:

> "The humble preaching of the Gospel and the administration of the simple Sacraments are the greatest things that can happen in the world. For in these things the hidden reign of Christ is consummated. He Himself is present in these means of grace, and the bearer of the ministry of the church actually stands in the stead of Christ. That certainly puts an end to any clerical conceit. We are nothing. He is everything." (Hermann Sasse, "The Lutheran Doctrine of the Office of the Ministry" in *The Lonely Way: II.* St. Louis: CPH 1992, p. 139)

"As it is written, 'How beautiful are the feet of those who preach the good news!'" (Romans 10:15) Preachers' feet are beautiful feet only because above them is an open mouth that proclaims the beautiful message of Christ and Him crucified, the Savior of sinners. That message, when heard and believed, makes for beautiful ears—the ears of faith. That message is based on something that once happened outside the beautiful city of Jerusalem. Who would have ever thought that outside that wondrous city there would be a battlefield called Calvary upon which the most decisive battle in world history would be fought? But there was. On it the crimson blood of God was shed to reconcile sinners to God and the skull of Satan was left crushed, giving preachers a message of triumph to preach that should make all ears everywhere tingle.

Letter 3 – Pastor as Visitor

Rev. Michael Daniels

In his book *The Hammer of God*, Bo Giertz begins with an account of a party that was happening amongst pastors and civic leaders. The party was interrupted by a messenger who came to get a pastor to come and attend to his brother-in-law who was on his deathbed. After some arguing and delaying, none of the pastors desired to leave the party and call on the dying man. Finally, the dean gave his command that the youngest pastor there would be the one to go and do the unwanted work. Although this is a fictional book, this is still the way that visitation is quite often thought of. Most pastors much prefer sitting in their comfortable offices studying, reading, and writing. Some churches even hire retired pastors to go and perform this unwanted work of visitation.

However, as difficult and as inconvenient as it may be, visitation is one of the most necessary and fulfilling tasks a pastor can do. It is something that is so important that it is even in the Rite of Ordination. Right after you vow not to divulge sins confessed to you the rite asks, "Will you minister faithfully to the sick and dying, and will you demonstrate to the Church a constant and ready ministry centered in the Gospel?" Not only is visitation a good thing to do, it is also something you vow to do in your ordination.

Though it may not be as glamorous as preaching a dynamite sermon to a packed house, going and visiting the sick and the shut-in is an important pastoral duty. While there are certainly elders and other members who are able to visit and encourage congregation members, it is the pastor who is Christ's representative. Just as you

stand in the stead of Christ in the chancel and declare the Absolution
and consecrate the Lord's Supper so also you stand in the stead of
Christ when you are there in the nursing home room or living room
of a shut-in member. You are bringing Jesus to them. In a wonderful
example of our weakness and inability you, as a pastor, are able to go
and quite literally meet them where they are. Just as Jesus sent the 72
to go and declare, "Peace be to this house!" so, too, He has sent you.
Not only has He sent you to preach and teach on His behalf in the
Church on Sunday morning, but He has also called you to go and
tend to those of His flock who are weak and struggling.

Unlike preaching or teaching Bible class, there are no deadlines
for shut-in calls, and so, quite often, if you are unmotivated, it is
difficult to make yourself go and do them. There are any number of
excuses and other things you feel you should attend to but visiting
shut-in sheep should be high on the list of priorities. True shut-ins are
incapable of being out and about and being present in the corporate
Divine Service so it is necessary for the pastor to bring the Divine
Service to them. These people are truly shut off from everyone else
and so it is necessary to go and give them the comfort and consolation
that only the Gospel can give. Also, quite often, they are hungrier to
hear it than your regular Sunday morning worshiper. No one is more
excited to see the pastor than the elderly shut-in who doesn't see
many other people and knows that his death has become ever closer.

To be at the deathbed of a faithful saint, to give her comfort and
consolation in the Gospel, is one of the greatest responsibilities a
pastor can have. Though it may not come at the time that you would
prefer, it is never an inconvenience to be there and shepherd a saint
through the portal to life immortal. At times, it can be emotional,
scary, messy, and even difficult, but there is always comfort in the
Gospel that we are given to proclaim. As pastors, we are with people
in some of the darkest times in their lives and can bring the light that
only Christ can give.

Pastors are also called to visit saints when they are sick and in
the hospital. Just as the physician cares for the aches and pains of the
body, the pastor cares for the aches and pains of the soul. As someone
and their loved ones are dealing with the anxieties and stresses that
illness brings, the pastor brings the healing words of the heavenly
Physician of both body and soul. As the suffering one is dealing in an

immediate way with the effects of our sinful fallen world, the pastor can proclaim the forgiveness of sins and comfort the conscience in a way no earthly medication can.

Though pastors are often thought of as being called for sad times when someone is sick or dying, they are also called to visit in times of joy and celebration. It is a wonderful privilege to be able to visit new families at the birth of their children and rejoice with them in the blessings that God gives. Pastors are also called on to visit people in their new homes and bless houses, that they would be a peaceful and Christian dwelling. As a pastor, you visit with people in the good and the bad and the mundane in-between.

Pastors can also benefit as much from visits as the members themselves. Quite often in the pastoral office we get weighed down by a lot of different issues and problems within the church. Visiting someone in need is a helpful reminder of the real reason that you are a pastor. When visiting, you aren't worried about the color of the carpet, or what the church council is doing or whatever trivial issue has arisen in the church. You are only concerned about bringing the Gospel to this one person or family. The distractions fade away and you are focused on the person in front of you and assuring them of the salvation that is there in Jesus Christ. Rather than trying to appeal to and connect with a whole congregation of people, you can directly address one person and the difficulty and hardship that they are enduring.

There are also times where certain members care for you as much as you care for them. Some are especially thoughtful and inquire how you and your family are doing, and really mean it. I can remember one lady I had the privilege of ministering to who would always manage to scrape together goody bags for my children on Easter and Christmas. And while things might not always be going the best in your congregation, it is always refreshing to see shut-ins and others who look forward to your visits.

Another occasion when pastors visit is when a member is in prison. As odd or as unusual as it may seem, it can be the case that a church member has some sort of transgression and is arrested. Though it isn't always easy and there are usually a lot of hoops to jump through, it is also important for a pastor to visit those in prison. Though they may have done some terrible things, they need to hear the Law and the Gospel as much as anyone. Quite often they are already convicted in the Law as their current location is a constant reminder to them. It is necessary that they hear the Gospel and the forgiveness that is there in Jesus. When we don't want to go, or despise those in prison, we would do well to remember the words of Jesus in the parable of the sheep and the goats. "'And when did we see you sick or in prison and visit you?' And the King will answer them, 'Truly, I say to you, as you did it to one of the least of these my brothers, you did it to me'" (Matthew 25:39-40).

Though it may not always be easy to want to visit those in prison, consider that you are doing this for Jesus Himself. Rather than seeing the sinful person that you are to visit, see Jesus. Don't see him as he is, see him as the Lord sees him—as someone who is clothed with the robe of Christ's righteousness that covers all his sin. While it may not seem fun to visit prisoners they are often just as excited to see you as anyone else is. They also typically thirst for the Gospel as much as anyone else does. In my own experience in prison ministry, those whom I have visited with don't have much else to do other than read the Bible and consider God's Word. I have had just as many interesting biblical discussions in a visitation room at the jail as I have elsewhere.

While it may be time consuming and seem less important than other things, make visitation a priority. Hold yourself accountable and repent when you haven't been as faithful and diligent as you should. Go and give Jesus to your people in the Means of Grace because they need it, and you will be glad that you did.

Letter 4 – Pastor as Forgiven Sinner

Rev. Dr. Roger C. Paavola

A close friend of mine, Dr. Johnson (not his actual name), was an orthopedic surgeon. We worked together in a large, busy metropolitan hospital. Before going to medical school, he was a collegiate football player, a lineman for a Division I football team, and he sustained a multitude of injuries while playing football all four years he was eligible. Those injuries, combined with the long hours he put in standing at an operating table, eventually led him to have a total knee replacement to remedy the issues of his legs and joints. He did the right thing by consulting a colleague and had his problems corrected with surgery. By receiving care from others when he needed it, this healer was able to continue his vocation of healing and being a blessing to others.

Pastors face a similar circumstance, and a similar "choice." We are worn down by our own record of sins, even as we routinely forgive the sins of others in Christ's stead. We're called by God to be *seelsorge*—someone who "treats" the affliction and consequences of what sin has done in a person's life. But what about the sin in our own lives? Unfortunately, sin is still an issue even after a pastor is ordained. The pastor absolves, but when is he absolved? No one can deny the mangled, twisted, and bruised ordeals the pastor will face. For clergy and laity alike, these things are caused by Satan, the world, and our own sinful selves, the consequences of living in a fallen world.

Yet, in God's divine providence, confession and Absolution of one's sins is a special Gift of God's grace not only for laity but also for the pastor. It is vital that the pastor repents of his sins, and knows

Christ's Absolution applies to him, too. Without God's Means of Grace, we can no longer stand. No pastor would tell a parishioner to shoulder the burden of his or her own sins, nor should he expect himself to do likewise. In His mercy, God has provided many ways for pastors to hear His Absolution, notably, in the liturgy of the historic Church.

In the Order of Compline (LSB 254), the pastor begins with these words: "I confess to God Almighty, before the whole company of heaven and to you, my brothers and sisters, that I have sinned in thought, word, and deed by my fault, by my own fault, by my own most grievous fault; wherefore I pray God Almighty to have mercy on me, forgive me all my sins, and bring me to everlasting life. Amen."

The congregants respond, "The almighty and merciful Lord grant you pardon, forgiveness, and remission of all your sins. Amen." These are especially sweet words, pronouncing God's grace to the pastor, who is also a poor, miserable sinner just like everyone else. God's grace and forgiveness of our sins is extended in mercy for the sake of our Savior, Jesus Christ. Compline reminds both the pastors and laity of the great Gift God offers in Christ.

Like all Christians, pastors need to hear the Gospel to strengthen them and keep them in the true faith. When a pastor does not hear the words of Absolution or take it to heart that the Gospel applies to him as well, his conscience is troubled. He may turn to his own works and piousness, or he may be driven towards despair and depression (or both). Martin Luther himself struggled with the gravity of sin as a young monk. He is quoted as saying during his monastic time, "I lost touch with Christ the Savior and Comforter, and made of him the jailer and hangman of my poor soul" (James Kittelson, *Luther The Reformer*, Minneapolis: Augsburg Fortress Publishing House, 1986, p. 79). Johann von Staupitz was Luther's father confessor. Staupitz pointed Luther away from his struggle with sinful unworthiness and brought him to hear the merits of Christ for the forgiveness of sin. Luther discovered that true redemption does not involve penance or self-inflicted punishments but rather depends wholly on the merits of Christ Jesus' redemptive work on our behalf.

Luther's "rediscovery" of the Gospel is clear: "But now the righteousness of God has been manifested apart from the law, although the Law and the Prophets bear witness to it—the righteousness of

God through faith in Jesus Christ for all who believe. For there is no distinction: for all have sinned and fall short of the glory of God, and are justified by his grace as a gift, through the redemption that is in Christ Jesus, whom God put forward as a propitiation by his blood, to be received by faith" (Romans 3:21-25).

As a pastor, Luther was convinced that only by God's grace alone, through faith alone, could anyone be at peace in the blessed assurance of forgiveness of sin for our eternal salvation. He wrote, "If now I seek the forgiveness of sins, I do not run to the cross, for I will not find it given there. Nor must I hold to the suffering of Christ, as Dr. Karlstadt trifles, in knowledge or remembrance, for I will not find it there either. But I will find in the sacrament or Gospel the word which distributes, presents, offers, and gives to me that forgiveness which was won on the cross" (*Luther's Works, Church and Ministry II*, ed. Jaroslav Jan Pelikan, Hilton C. Oswald, and Helmut T. Lehmann, vol. 40, p. 214).

This is the Gospel proclamation's source and substance that we pronounce. We are reminded that not only does it apply to our hearers, but it must also apply to us, the pastors who proclaim the Gospel. As Lutheran pastors, we remain understudies of the Great Physician who has entrusted us with the care of people's souls unto eternal salvation. The principal responsibilities of the pastoral office are perilous work if not taken seriously. Hebrews 13 reminds the pastor that he is to give an account of his stewardship of the Office—both Law and Gospel—now and on the Last Day. If a pastor fails to care for those under his ministry and neglects to proclaim the Gospel of the forgiveness of sin that offers eternal life, to his parishioners and to himself (the pastor is not exempt from the congregation!), he is held accountable before the Lord God.

The apostle James wrote, "Let not many of you become teachers, my brethren, knowing that as such we shall incur a stricter judgment" (James 3:1, NASB). Of course, left on our own, with the care of souls given to our charge, we would face a humbling terror over our own inadequacy for the task. But here are the comforting words of the quintessential pastor, Paul: "Not that we are sufficient in ourselves to claim anything as coming from us, but our sufficiency is from God, who has made us sufficient to be ministers of a new covenant, not of the letter but of the Spirit. For the letter kills, but the Spirit gives life" (2 Corinthians 3:5-6). Pastors are totally dependent on Him who supplies and equips His undershepherds for the task to which He has called us. This applies not only to proclaiming the Gospel to our flock, but also to ourselves.

Jesus uses a common Jewish phrase, "Physician, heal thyself" in Luke 4:23 (KJV). It was believed that before a physician could adequately cure another person's disease, he must heal himself first. My orthopedic surgeon friend, Dr. Johnson, would never have been foolish enough to perform a total knee replacement on himself! He had to trust that procedure to a colleague who would complete the task safely, completely, and properly. By the same token, the pastor should not only dutifully declare the forgiveness of sins, but he must also believe and live, knowing the Great Physician will forgive his sins as well.

Our pastoral responsibility drives us toward total dependence on God-supplied sufficiency. Just as Dr. Johnson sought another qualified surgeon to do his knee replacement, pastors should also avail themselves of the "scalpel of God's Word" to bring their confession before a brother-confessor. The sweet sound of Absolution must echo in the pastor's ears as well; "In the stead and by the command of my Lord, Jesus Christ, and by His authority, I forgive you of all your sins, in the name of the Father, and of the Son (+), and of the Holy Spirit . . . Now may the God of peace Himself sanctify you completely, and may your whole spirit, soul, and body be blameless at the coming of our Lord Jesus Christ. He who calls you is faithful; He will surely do it. Go in (+) peace." Amen.

Just as Dr. Johnson was able to return to the operating suite after a short time of rehabilitation to continue his work of enabling his patients to return to their own normal physical activity, pastors burdened with the enormity of their own sinfulness, through confession and Absolution as a Means of God's Grace, can return to their pastoral duties, freed from the debilitating impairment caused by sin. Thanks be to God for His tender grace and mercy.

Letter 5 – Pastor as Student of Theology

Rev. Aaron T. Fenker

I want to let you know, it's the difficult path. There's nothing you can do to make it any easier. It's rocky, bumpy, and topsy-turvy. "What makes it so difficult?" you ask. It's not the path of giving. No, it's the path of receiving. This is something our flesh never wants to do.

The path of being a theologian is receiving from Jesus, receiving His Word. It's more His Word FOR YOU and less of your own FROM YOU. To be a pastor and a student of theology is to be a student of the Scriptures, sitting, as it were, at the nail-scarred feet of Jesus, hearing and receiving Jesus' Word—all of His Word—as Gift.

It's an impossible task, job, to-do list. Impossible for you, but not impossible with Jesus. What you can't possibly do, He impossibly delivers to you over and over again, deep and deeper still, all the way to the end, then back to the beginning, rinse and repeat. He gives to you, steeping you, filling you, overflowing you with His Word, that His Word would become your word in preaching, teaching, and caring for the people He gives you.

You, as a pastor, will be the cross, the intersection, the place where the Scriptures and suffering meet, where the Spirit-filled Law and Gospel and sins meet, where Jesus and sinners meet. That place is the crucible of theology. For wherever and whenever Christ crucified meets our crosses and suffering and sins with His peace and forgiveness, that's where theology is made. In those situations, the Spirit shapes, informs, and fills with the Scriptures our words about who God is for you, how He's disposed towards you in Christ Jesus. *Crux sola est nostra Theologia.* "The cross alone is our theology," as Luther put it.

Being a theologian, a biblical theologian, is rejoicing in the gifts of the languages, too. Studying the original languages delivers insight. There is gift in the translations, too. Pentecost tells us the Gospel is for all peoples, nations, languages, and tongues (Revelation 7:9). For, they "all heard them in their own tongues telling the mighty works of God" (Acts 2:11) in Christ Jesus. Yet, while the Spirit is in the preaching of the Gospel (Romans 10), He inspired (2 Timothy 3:16) Paul's Greek, Moses' Hebrew, and Daniel's Aramaic, just to name a few.

Your ministry and delivery of God's Word to His saints will involve both your heart and your mind. So also your devotions and worship: "For if I pray in a tongue, my spirit prays but my mind is unfruitful. What am I to do? I will pray with my spirit, but I will pray with my mind also; I will sing praise with my spirit, but I will sing with my mind also" (1 Corinthians 14:14-15). Thus English (or whatever language you will preach and teach in) and the original languages are the Spirit's tool to bless your heart, soul, mind, and strength to deliver the Good News of what Jesus has done for you and for all.

What about theology? There's that gift, too. What is theology but confessing? How to do the theology of the Scriptures, how to confess them, is taught to you by the *Lutheran Confessions.* You will make them your confession. Learn from them: their exegesis, their doctrine, the other theological works to which they would point you, too. The preaching, teaching, and confessing of the *Lutheran Confessions* will preach, teach, and confess you into being a true Lutheran pastor.

You'll learn how theology isn't just for the ivory tower, but for the troubled conscience, for the deathbed. Luther, the primary teacher of our church, along with Melanchthon, Chemnitz, Andreae, and the other Formulators of Concord, will convince you that the chief doctrine, the chief teaching of this church is this: your forgiveness, your innocent verdict (justification) before God is on account of Christ's merits alone, all received by faith alone. Justification by grace through faith is the article by which your ministry will stand or fall, as it is with the whole Church of God in Christ Jesus.

No matter which doctrine is confessed by you as a Lutheran pastor, the *Book of Concord* will teach you that it all centers on Christ as your only Savior from sin, death, and the power of the devil. So, rejoice in the confessions. Preach and teach the *Small Catechism* to your people, connect it to the *Large Catechism*, the *Augsburg Confession*, the *Apology*, the *Smalcald Articles*, the *Formula of Concord*. Forward and back again, front to back, rinse and repeat. You may just be a halfway decent theologian when you don your stole for the last time.

What about other theologians? What about reading Gerhard or Pieper, Athanasius or Augustine, Walther or Nagel, or any other living theologians? They are a gift for you, too. As they were ministers of the Gospel, their crosses are your cross. Their people's crosses are your people's crosses. The vanities we chase, the evil we experience, the doubts we wrestle with are the same from age to age. As Solomon says of such things, "There is nothing new under the sun" (Ecclesiastes 1:9).

So, read those theologians, too. Their faithfully confessing the Scriptures (their theologizing, their preaching, their exegeting, their praying) is a blessing to you. They will teach you, guide you in how to take up the task of being a theologian—confessing the Scriptures, doing theology, preaching, exegeting, teaching, praying. But beware, as Solomon also says, "The words of the wise are like goads, and like nails firmly fixed are the collected sayings; they are given by one Shepherd. My son, beware of anything beyond these. Of making many books there is no end, and much study is a weariness of the flesh" (Ecclesiastes 12:11-12). Even Luther himself wished most of his books to be burned so that those after him would not set aside the Scriptures.

But the true lamp to your feet isn't the theologians. "Your Word is a Lamp to my feet and a light to my path" (Psalm 119:105). Only the Scriptures can do that. Sure, the theologians confess the doctrines expressed in the Scriptures, but they are no substitute for what the Spirit Himself would teach you from His Word. The theologians can be a faithful witness to our one Scriptural faith, but they ought not supplant the Scriptures.

Those faithful theologians are important. Their confession is important. But you will not make their confession your own. In your ordination vows, you will only join the *Book of Concord* to yourself, and yourself to the *Book of Concord* in that way.

I know from experience how tempting and easy it is to use theologians as shorthand for proper biblical study. In fact, I've often found that I can anticipate the texts and exegesis of our Lutheran forefathers. This isn't necessarily because I've studied them in depth, although that is a good gift. It's actually because of the Scriptures themselves! (Same goes for the *Lutheran Confessions*, too.)

Please, don't misunderstand me here. I'm not boasting in my own ability, but rather I'm boasting in what the Spirit Himself does through the Word! His Word is living and active (Hebrews 4:12). His Word makes us holy in the Truth (John 17:19). "'But the Helper, the Holy Spirit, whom the Father will send in my name, he will teach you all things and bring to your remembrance all that I have said to you'" (John 14:26).

Paul's words are true for all pastors, as they were true to young pastor Timothy: "Keep a close watch on yourself and on the teaching. Persist in this, for by so doing you will save both yourself and your hearers" (1 Timothy 4:16).

Does all this sound like a lot? It is. It means early mornings, or late nights. Sometimes, it's some of both! But the Lord's Word will enliven you to the task. At whatever point, or whatever time you find yourself, there is Jesus, by His Holy-Spirit filled Word, making you a theologian, a proper student of theology, a proper disciple. As Luther said, "Let no one think he has sufficiently grasped the Holy Scriptures, unless he has governed the churches for 100 years."

It is, after all, the difficult path. There's nothing you can do to make it any easier. It's rocky, bumpy, and topsy-turvy. "What makes it so difficult?" you ask. It's not the path of giving. No, it's the path of receiving.

The path of being a theologian is receiving from Jesus, receiving His Word. It's more His Word FOR YOU and less of your own FROM YOU. To be a pastor and a student of theology is to be a student of the Scriptures, sitting, as it were, at the nail-scarred feet of Jesus, hearing and receiving Jesus' Word, all of His Word, as Gift.

Letter 6 – Pastor in Society

Rev. Dr. Gregory P. Seltz

I've been thinking a lot about you lately. You've known the exhilaration of competition, of good sportsmanship, and teamwork. Your peers consider you to be a leader. You have excelled in your school-work through effort and sacrifice and now you have important decisions to make regarding your future. This is such a special moment in your life, yet I do remember how overwhelming and/or confusing it can be. Indeed, there is much confusion in the chaos of today's world. As I write this, I'm sitting in my office in Washington, D.C., looking back on a ministry that has spanned over 35 years in places such as New York City, Los Angeles, and Dallas. Sometimes I wonder how I've gotten to this place. What I can say is that God has a plan for me, and I know that He has a plan for you, too.

One of the greatest joys is finding your life's purpose and consequently making decisions that serve and honor God. Perhaps you are contemplating colleges and weighing a variety of majors, vocations, careers, or other opportunities that you feel might be "calling" you and tugging at your heart strings. This is an important milestone for you. Or maybe you are already in college, knee-deep in your studies.

Yet, while you are enjoying learning and the overall college atmosphere, something else seems to be pulling at you. Maybe you are feeling forces on campus tearing you away from your first love, your love of your Lord and Savior Jesus. Maybe it's gnawing at you because you sense that you're being pulled toward things that you know are not better things.

Such was my experience over 40 years ago. Ironically, amidst my dream opportunities at the University of Michigan, I found a higher calling demanding my best. Today, I'm thinking that God might be calling you to imagine what He could accomplish through you for others. I'm wondering if you have pondered the possibility of being a pastor in the Lutheran Church–Missouri Synod where you would strive for excellence as a leader in Christ's Church.

The Bible says that a desire to serve in this capacity is a very good thing. The apostle Paul himself says, in 1 Timothy 3:1, "The saying is trustworthy: If anyone aspires to the office of overseer, he desires a noble task." The ESV translates the office of overseer as a "noble task." Others translate it, "a good work," or, "a good thing."

Reflecting on the cultural challenges facing those in pastoral ministry today, I would add that it is a very "courageous thing" as well. In fact, if you desire the work of sharing the whole counsel of God as a pastor today, I would describe it as the "hardest, greatest work that you will ever love."

When I was privileged to train urban, church-planting pastors in my ministry, I shared with them that they had to be the best theologians, Bible scholars, and evangelists of and for the Church. They had to strive to be "Navy SEALs for Christ," those with the mindset that nothing in this world would deter them from the mission that Jesus wants His pastors to do. The "pastoral calling of publicly sharing God's Law and God's Gospel so that people might indeed be saved" is a message that is needed now more than ever.

That is why I pray that you would think deeply about the calling of being a leader in and for Christ's Church. Let me be as straightforward as I can be. As I write, many say that we are in the throes of a culture war. It's true. The Christian worldview is not only under attack, but also is now seen as an impediment to progress. Virtually all the "systems" of our culture—the educational, the political, the cultural, and even the economic institutions—eye the things of God with suspicion, if they even entertain them at all. God's moral ordering of the world is now seen as bigoted and hateful. Even the uniqueness of Christ's salvation FOR ALL, is perceived as intolerant of our varied personal views of autonomy and self-determination. Many are discouraged, claiming that the culture war is lost.

Today, we need "Navy SEALs For Christ" pastors who know that it's never been whether we are winning or losing the culture wars, but whether we are engaging it with the whole counsel of God for the sake of our culture and our people. We need pastors who know that God is still at work in the world, preserving it so that He might offer His saving Word as a Gift. "Render to Caesar what is Caesar's and to God what is God's" (Mark 12:17) still applies, and pastors need to be able to differentiate such work for the sake of the mission of the Church like never before.

I pray that today you don't just hear some "seasoned pastor" trying to persuade you towards this high calling, but God Himself. I pray that He impresses upon you the needs to be faced as well as the opportunities that only He can provide. God's people need faithful, committed, courageous, empathetic, speakers-of-God's-truth-in-love, those who would joyfully lead and encourage His flock. People need leaders with the conviction of Daniel, of Shadrach, Meshach, Abednego, and Esther, who are willing to stand, to serve, and to lead "for such a time as this" (Esther 4:14). And those outside of God's Church need authentic voices of His salt and light, offering them a "beyond their imagination" message of grace that is freely offered to people like you, like them, for all.

Let me encourage you today to consider this calling! I've seen first-hand what our God can do through His ministry (sometimes even in spite of ourselves). He is the Savior; you and I, the servant-leaders. He is the Message, we are the "mouthpieces" through whom He speaks. He is the promise given and the promise fulfilled which animates our work even as it radiates through us to others.

Yes, He can still do great things for others through people like you and me. In today's chaotic reality I've seen it in the cities and the communities that I've served. I've seen God at work in people's living rooms, hospital rooms, and board rooms. I've seen the power of faith at work in the poorest people in the community and the spirit of repentance and faith among the richest, and vice-versa. I've shared the transforming Good News of Jesus on the radio, on the television, and in quiet, deeply personal conversations in people's backyards. And one thing that I have come to know about being Christ's pastor for others is that, often in spite of us, God can bring people to faith in Him through the power of His Gifts—His Word and His Sacraments—especially when pastors are courageous enough to bring it to whomever God calls them to serve.

If this is indeed the direction you are considering . . . you desire a noble work, a good work, and a courageous work for times such as these. Let me also say that you desire a work that God Himself promises to sustain, to empower, even to bless. In Philippians 3:10-11, Paul reflects on the power of faith in Christ and the goal of such leading and serving. He says, "that I may know him and the power of his resurrection, and may share his sufferings, becoming like him in his death, that by any means possible I may attain the resurrection from the dead." Wow, what a calling! If you desire to serve, to lead, and to deliver His Good News on His Law/Gospel terms, you will see the answer to that desire in the work of ministry, especially in the world in which we live today. Join us. Become a "Navy SEAL for Christ" in service to His Church. You'll be blessed if you do.

Letter 7 – Pastor as a Student of Scripture

Rev. Christopher Neuendorf

Before I became a pastor, I would think about what I really wanted in my own pastor, and therefore what sort of pastor *I* would hope to become. What I most wanted in my pastor was a student of Scripture. I wanted to know that if I had a question about some biblical teaching, I could go to my pastor and receive from him sound guidance in understanding and applying the Bible. I wanted a pastor who would not be confused by the clever arguments of the skeptics, and who, if he didn't know the answer off the top of his head, would at least know where to look to find it. Of course, there are many things that a Christian wants in a pastor, but every desirable pastoral characteristic will be amplified if the pastor is, first and foremost, a student of Scripture, which is to say, a disciple of Jesus Christ.

To be a pastor is to be a student of Scripture. This is true of the pastor simply as a Christian, as a professional, and as one under affliction. In each case, God uses the pastor's study of Scripture to form him into a servant who will be a blessing to those under his care.

Every Christian is to be a student of Scripture (2 Timothy 3:15). Of course, Christians study the Scriptures by attentive participation in the regular services of the Church. Hearing the lessons read and expounded upon in the context of the Divine Service is the foundational lifelong instruction on which every Christian is nourished. Since the advent of print, however, and the availability of reliable translations in the vernacular, every Christian has the opportunity for daily meditation in the Scriptures. Daily devotion in the form of prayer and Scripture study is an indispensable part of the Christian life. Omit this, and your faith will suffer. This is as true for the pastor as it is for the lay Christian.

Ideally, the pastor will set aside time every day to read the Bible in the context of prayer. When it comes to daily Scripture study, my recommendation is to follow a yearly reading plan and read the Bible right through from cover to cover annually, in translation. I cannot emphasize enough the blessing of repeated reading of the entirety of Holy Scripture. The student of Scripture who does this will find himself truly learning the Scriptures forwards and backwards. He will make connections between passages that would otherwise never have occurred to him. Seemingly obscure passages will rise to the fore of his consciousness at the most opportune times. The language and thought patterns of Scripture will become his own.

Whatever reading pattern the pastor settles on for himself, these daily readings can begin with prayer for the Holy Spirit, whom our Father in heaven will not withhold from those who ask Him (Luke 11:13), and it is through the Word being read that the Spirit is given. Following the Scripture reading, the pastor can pray as he is stirred by what he has just read. There are plenty of sound devotional resources that will assist the pastor in being a daily devotional student of Scripture, simply as a Christian.

The pastor, however, is more than simply a Christian. He is also a professional, who earns his daily bread by instructing in the Word those fellow Christians entrusted to his care (1 Timothy 5:18; Galatians 6:6). As such, the pastor has a responsibility to do more than the most basic devotional study of Holy Scripture. The pastor can study the Scriptures in their original languages, he can profitably consult in-depth commentaries, and he can set limits upon his own speculations through the study of the *Lutheran Confessions* and other sound doctrinal writings of our church. He can set aside office time for this every morning with a good conscience, knowing that this is one of the chief things his people are paying him to do.

One of the most valuable tools acquired by the pastor during his education is the ability to work with Greek and Hebrew. The pastor owes it to his flock to keep his linguistic skills at their best. He should regularly review his grammars, and he should read daily in the Hebrew Old Testament and the Greek New Testament. This will be a much closer study than that which is engaged in devotionally. He will want to ensure that he has a firm grasp of the meaning that the Holy Spirit wishes to convey through the biblical text.

Often, of course, the pastor may be left wondering more about a passage even after consulting lexical and grammatical resources. For these occasions, he is equipped with the necessary skills to make profitable use of technical commentaries. If he can afford it, the volumes of the *Concordia Commentary* series will be invaluable to him. He should also be on the lookout for local retiring pastors who are liquidating their libraries; countless gems for the study of Scripture can be acquired at such opportunities. Furthermore, in our information age, you can nearly always track down what you need to find the best current answer to the trickiest questions of interpretation. There are plentiful older commentaries available through such resources as Google Books and internet archives. The *Keil and Delitzsch Commentary* remains a fantastic series for Old Testament study from an orthodox Lutheran perspective and can be found in full online. Interlibrary loan through your local public library can give you access to more recent aids without breaking the bank. Even commentaries that contain much chaff can be of value, especially as the pastor has been alerted through his training to the pitfalls of higher criticism, though this should always be undertaken with care and humility, taking heed lest he fall (1 Corinthians 10:12). The pastor should approach this task with fear and trembling, in godly subjection to the Lord of the Church.

To this end, I recommend that the pastor set bounds to his in-depth study by regular reading of the *Book of Concord*, thus hewing to the pattern of sound words (2 Timothy 1:13). I have found that the more I read the *Lutheran Confessions*, the more impressed I am by the Reformers' exegetical acumen. Likewise, the more I read the Scriptures themselves, the more I recognize the teachings of the Bible in the *Lutheran Confessions*. A thorough grounding in our confessions can serve as a valuable safeguard against the excesses of those biblical commentators who might otherwise lead us astray.

By such a grasp of the biblical languages, recent scholarship in the form of commentaries, and the doctrinal grounding of the *Lutheran Confessions*, the pastor in his capacity as a professional student of Scripture will prove a great blessing to those under his care who wish to grow in the knowledge of Scripture themselves.

There is, however, one further way in which the pastor becomes a student of Scripture for his own blessing and for the blessing of his people. This further form of study is involuntary. As a Christian, the pastor intentionally sets aside time every day for the devotional reading of Scripture. As a professional, he intentionally maintains and uses his linguistic and research skills to grow in his understanding of Scripture. But it is as one afflicted that the pastor is forced to the study of Scripture for his very survival.

Before I became a pastor, I recognized the Scriptures as a refuge in times of trouble. But it was only after I began to bear the burden of preaching, of ministering to those in distress, and of suffering attacks from those whom the Word of God has confronted through my ministry that I actually found myself driven to Holy Scripture. It is in these cases that Scripture ceases to be an object of voluntary study and becomes a most necessary solace, meat and drink, a sweet salve and healing balm. It has been those moments when God has especially used His Word to conform me closer to the image of Christ (Romans 8:29). The pastor who has been thus formed through the trial of affliction and the comfort of the Scriptures is prepared to be a blessing to his people.

Being enriched by the study of Scripture in all these ways leads to inexpressible blessing for the pastor. The saving truth of the Bible will well up in his preaching of its own accord. His prayers will be suffused with the patterns of speech and thought that characterize the Bible. He will be able to hold his own in his opposition to the enemies of God's Word and God's people. May the Lord of the Church grant us such pastors—and may He make you such a pastor.

Letter 8 – Pastor as a Student of Hymnody

Rev. Gary W. Schultz

Hymnody is doctrine in practice. With rhyme and meter, hymn writers proclaim the counsel of our Lord in poetic form. Musicians set these poems to pitches and rhythms. Sometimes the words are written first. Sometimes a hymn writer has a tune in mind and fits the text to the tune. Occasionally, the author of the text and composer of the tune are the same person. Pastors study all of this, from the hymns of the early Church to the hymns of today, with a special focus on the core hymns of our Lutheran confession, the hymns of the Reformation, and the period of Lutheran orthodoxy.

Our hymns tell interesting stories. Often they reflect or hint at situations going on at the time of their writing: from bad times (wars, plagues, depression, or death) to good times (celebrations, thanksgivings, births, and marriages).

Our hymns mark time. Medieval office hymns form the foundation of our hymnody and sing of every time of day and night and every season of the liturgical year. Following this lead, Lutheran hymn writers also wrote hymns to commemorate the seasons of the year (Advent, Christmas, Epiphany, Lent, Easter, Pentecost, Trinity, to the End Times and back again) and days commemorating saints (apostles and evangelists) and events in the life of Jesus (Presentation, Annunciation, etc.).

Pastors are students of hymnody because hymnody is a vital tool in the pastor's arsenal. It is an important part of the pastor's life of prayer, study, catechesis, and visitation. Hymns are part of pastoral care in times of celebration, times of trial, and the daily rhythm of life.

Hymns are a part of the pastor's daily prayer. First and foremost, the pastor sings hymns as part of his individual or family prayer each morning and evening. The repetition of strong hymns year after year supports the singing of the liturgy of the Daily Office (Matins and Vespers) and the reading of Scripture, sermons, and meditations. Hymns as a regular part of daily prayer fortify the pastor for his care of the souls in his parish and for spreading God's Word in the community. Even more essentially, hymns are an ongoing reminder of the truths of God's Word for a pastor's own life of faith. In our parish, we encourage the singing of a hymn each month that will be the hymn of the day in an upcoming Divine Service.

Hymns are a part of the pastor's regular study. It is beneficial for the pastor to make the singing of the hymn of the day and other hymns written on the texts of the lectionary (or for a particular day or season of the Church year) part of preparation for writing sermons and studying the themes of the upcoming Sunday. As pastors prepare Bible study, they consider how hymns could be part of reinforcing the lesson. When writing a sermon, I will often sing the hymn of the day scheduled for that occasion, and sometimes a phrase or a stanza will work its way into the sermon.

Hymns are part of the pastor's catechesis. This includes those going through organized catechetical instruction preparing for reception of the Lord's Supper or to become members of the church, as well as for the ongoing instruction in the Christian faith. Especially as pastors instruct in the Six Chief Parts of Luther's *Small Catechism*, they will benefit from leading their catechumens in the singing of Luther's catechism hymns. When pastors instruct those who have not grown up in the Church, hymns are an easy and memorable way to reinforce distinctly Lutheran teaching.

Hymns are also a part of the pastor's work of visitation. When visiting members in the hospital, at the nursing home, or at the home following a tragedy or its anniversary, hymns are tools that may be employed to provide comfort and counsel from the Word of God in a memorable way. The pastor as a student of hymnody can call to mind an appropriate hymn; or, in a pinch, if his mind is distracted, he can open to the "trust," "hope and comfort," or appropriate season of the Church year sections of the hymnal and start singing. It amazes me how often the hymn I've chosen—whether knowingly or not—relates to the difficult situation in which I've been called to guide and comfort my members and their families. I cannot count the times when I have prayed the prayers, lessons, and psalms from the *Pastoral Care Companion*, but it seems premature to leave, so I intersperse the silence or conversation with hymns.

Luther wrote that prayer, meditation, and affliction (*oratio, meditatio, tentatio*) make a theologian. Part of a pastor being prepared for this task is why he is a student of hymnody. The pastor sings hymns in prayer and studies them in his preparation for preaching and teaching so that he might use them in dealing with his own affliction and in the suffering and testing of those he serves in his parish, his brother pastors, or whomever he meets in the world.

Perhaps Christians are the most familiar with hymns as part of Divine Service on Sundays and Feasts. Here, the pastor's role as student of hymnody is important [1] to support the proclamation of the Word of God and celebration of the Lord's Supper; [2] to exhort parishioners to use their hymnals at home, to sing the strong hymns used in Divine Service as part of daily prayer and catechesis in the home.

The pastor is a student of hymnody because he must take a proactive role in leading the church in solid, biblical, confessional Lutheran hymns. For many parishioners, sometimes even life-long Lutherans, many Lutheran hymns remain unfamiliar. There is a continual need for encouragement and teaching to lead or strengthen Christians in our rich treasury of Lutheran hymns.

The pastor as a student of hymnody is a life-long process. The lives and stories of hymn writers, hymn composers, translators, editors—as well as hymnals, versions, and variations—is boundless. There are new hymns and tunes being written, and new hymns and tunes to write. A good place to start is the hymns of Martin Luther, many of which remain unfamiliar in our parishes. Luther's hymns are important to explore for three reasons: [1] they utilize a number of different sources, like medieval Latin hymns and German folk hymns, combined with new material, written during a time of urgency to teach Christian doctrine; [2] they fall into a number of categories to help organize various types of hymns (catechism hymns, Church year hymns, paraphrases of liturgy, and Psalm paraphrases); [3] they set the stage for other Reformers to write hymns and other musical material that led to the Lutheran confession being called "the singing church."

After becoming familiar with the hymns of Luther, consider the life and work of Paul Gerhardt, one of the greatest hymn writers of all time. From there, you can go in endless directions to enjoy the fascinating story of our hymns. It is both a historical journey and preparation for pastoral service.

With 500 years of Lutheran hymn writers building upon a heritage extending back to the days of the early Church, one could be tempted to think there is nothing new to say about hymns, or no new hymns to write. But the story is an ongoing part of our heritage. My mentor, Kantor Richard Resch, wrote a beautiful hymn, "The Gifts Christ Freely Gives" (LSB 602) in 2001 that fills a unique place for extolling the Means of Grace in a way no other hymn does. These Gifts to Christ's Church are distributed in Holy Baptism (stanza 2), Absolution (stanza 3), the Word of God (stanza 4), and the Lord's Supper (stanza 5), with a conclusion of praise and sound doctrine (stanza 6). And you never know: Being a student of hymnody might lead *you* to contribute to our Lutheran musical heritage.

Christ's blessings to you in your journey as a student of hymnody.

Letter 9 – Pastor as a Student of Liturgy

Rev. Sean Daenzer

Jesus says, "If you abide in my word, you are truly my disciples, and you will know the truth, and the truth will set you free" (John 8:31-32). When He says this, He does not intend that you ever get beyond being His disciple. He calls you to "remain and live constantly with" that Word, as a life-long student. Before anyone is a pastor in Christ's Church, you are a disciple. You remain a disciple even if you take up another office or duty. If ever you cease to be a disciple, you would cease to be a Christian.

When I urge you to become a disciple of the liturgy, then, I don't only mean that you should study and read something about worship. I mean just as our Lord means when He says, "Abide in My Word." Begin and remain a student of the liturgy your whole life long.

I do not say this because the study of liturgy is greater or even equal to the Word of God—in our churches nothing is of higher or equal authority to the prophetic and apostolic Scriptures. Rather, I urge you to become a student of the liturgy precisely because the liturgy, in its greatest part, is nothing other than the Word of God. This is the first and greatest benefit of the Lutheran liturgy, that in it the Word of Christ dwells richly among us (Colossians 3:16).

The services of the Lutheran church are so full of God's Word that you may overlook it. In the first place, we do something simple that many Protestants have abandoned: we read portions of the Bible, free of any human commentary. We hear from the prophets in the

Old Testament, from the apostles in their Epistles, and from Christ Himself in the Holy Gospel. In many other churches, the only time the Bible is heard is when it is quoted during the leader's message.

In the second place, the Scriptures fill every gap in between as well. Scarcely a moment passes when a psalm verse is not spoken or sung. Even the most common, seemingly "dispensable" parts of our services are invariably another passage from the Bible. So richly does the Word of God dwell in our service that we have "Scripture to spare," as it were. (More on this later.)

In the third place, by means of the liturgy the Christian's shelves are stocked with staples, without which no soul dares live (or die). The canticles of the Divine Service are not an exercise in vain repetition. They arm us with the Scriptures for life and death: the sinner's prayer in the "Kyrie eleison" (Luke 18:13); the great sermon of John the Baptist, "Behold, the Lamb of God who takes away the sin of the world" (John 1:29); the biblical confession of the faithful departing in Simeon's song (Luke 2:29ff); and the glimpse into eternity and rehearsal for the Last Day in the angel's acclamation, "Holy Lord God of Sabaoth" (Isaiah 6:3). To these also are added the Words of Institution and the Lord's Prayer, so that no Lutheran is without a crystal-clear statement of the Gospel and sure words to address his heavenly Father.

The difficult task is to find what is not God's Word in the Lutheran liturgy. The Apostles' Creed? A summary of the whole Bible. The sermon? Woe to the preacher who brings his own words (Jeremiah 23:28)! The hymns and prayers? Human poetry to be sure, but in our church the subject matter must be Divine. For two millennia the Scriptures have given rise to prayer and praise. They are still yielding their riches (Matthew 13:52). For this reason I dare to say, "Be a student of this liturgy," that is, of the forms and patterns, rites and ceremonies, hymns and chants of our church's services. In them, for generations now, Paul's admonition has been heeded. The Word of Christ dwells richly in the heritage of the Christian centuries. And you, if you would be wise, may gain divine wisdom beyond your years, receiving the faith once delivered to the saints (Jude 1:3) as it has steadily been delivered to the saints who followed them.

You wish to be the Lord's disciple, so you must abide at His feet and listen to Him in His Word. If you aspire to the office of overseer, that noble task (1 Timothy 3:1), then all the more you must sit, as the true prophets did, in the counsel of God (Jeremiah 23:18). You must devote yourself to the public reading of the Scriptures (1 Timothy 4:13) and to the Ministry of the Word (Acts 6:4). You must remain a hearer (and a believer) of the Word you would preach.

It is easy for the noble task to become perfunctory, especially in preparation for preaching. As a pastor, I, even more than my people, easily become bored with it. The day comes when I say, "I am tired of preaching on this text." It is important to recognize that this boredom is my sin. I am bored with the life-giving Word, which cannot be that Word's fault. My familiarity is no reason for contempt—how familiar with it am I really? The accompanying temptation to sloth is usually restlessness: to overcome boredom not with deeper attention, but with distraction. I may be tempted to depart from the lectionary, the hymns, the liturgy—to abandon the discipline. Will I be surprised when my hearers abandon it also (Hebrews 10:25)?

The discipline I'm advocating for is really to return our attention to our duties and to the unseen realities to which our office is devoted. It is the very discipline we seek to inspire in the saints also. To be sure, we want them in Bible class, regular home devotions, and any number of catechism and prayer habits, with every good work that arises from them. Nevertheless, "going to church" will never stop being the most fundamental mark and activity of a Christian—as it should be, for the branches must receive their nourishment from their true Vine (John 15:5).

Pastors must not merely "do" church services; we must "go to church" ourselves, for ourselves (1 Timothy 4:16; Acts 20:28). I said that in the liturgy we have "Scriptures to spare." Thanks be to God, not everything of our most holy faith is grasped and finished in a moment. There is always something more to abide in for life. When we receive and sit under the pattern of sound words in the Lutheran liturgy, we will learn and recognize new connections and delights from the Word of God that we did not see in previous years. We will come to love and expect the Sundays of the year with their hymns. We will learn to apply them to the conscience, "teaching and admonishing one another in all wisdom" (Colossians 3:16).

In your study, then, be patient. Grow into a faith and practice that is bigger than you. Likewise, expect that treasures old and new will arise from abiding in the Lord's Word. This attention will show in your conduct of the service. Others will see that you are not just "doing your job," but are yourself engaged in the church's life which comes from Christ's Word and blessed Sacraments.

In closing, here is some practical advice for you as a student of the liturgy. Begin with the service book you have. The goal is that you no longer need to open it. In general, be wary of oversimplifications about what "the Church has always done." At the same time, while "this is how we've always done it" may be a terrible excuse, it is sometimes an honest and even sufficient reason to continue. As a student, I advise you to remain quick to care about why we do what we do and slow to decide you know better.

Learn the rubrics. Having and observing liturgical rules does not make you a legalist. Obsessing over them might. Inevitably, you will depart from them in some way. This is far more tolerable when you know you have done so—and can answer "why." Christian worship may be simple, but it must be reverent. Reverence as a pastor is most directly a function of preparation, as a Christian, of evangelical faith.

Sing as much as possible and learn to sing well. In hymnody, treasure the Latin, Luther, and Gerhard hymns best of all. Learn them by heart and sing them especially when you fear someone might find it strange. Become a student of your church musician, and you will be rewarded.

Last of all, do not be ashamed that you are Lutheran. You are free to receive and use the full 2000 years of Christian life and history without apology. You are free to reject whatever runs contrary to the Scriptures, whether of recent or ancient origin. And if you ever believe you are the only student of the liturgy, do not look elsewhere for inspiration or perfection. Permit the Lutheran teaching and Christian heritage to animate your services and your life. Whatever our tradition might lack, it is not the Word of God's truth rightly divided. You are Christ's disciple, abiding in His Word. You are "ἐλεύθερος" (eleutheros)—free indeed.

Letter 10 – Pastor at Prayer

Rev. Dr. John T. Pless

The road of formation for future pastors requires not only diligent study but also prayer. This is recognized in the Rite of Ordination where the congregation is reminded that the candidate has prepared himself for the sacred responsibilities of the Office of the Holy Ministry by prayer and careful study. Prayer will also be an ongoing component of the pastoral office as the candidate pledges himself to continue in his study of the Holy Scriptures, the *Lutheran Confessions*, and to be constant in prayer for those committed to his care.

I am writing this "letter of encouragement" to invite and encourage you to initiate a regular pattern of prayer in light of your aspiration to the preaching office. The pattern I am commending to you is an old one. It goes back to Martin Luther and it consists of three Latin terms that I'll unpack in this letter: *oratio*, *meditatio*, and *tentatio*. Before I do that, let me give you a little information about the background and context of Luther's crafting of these three "touchstones" as he called them.

In 1539, Luther prepared a preface for the Wittenberg Edition of his German writings (you may read the entire piece in *The Annotated Luther, Vol. 4: Pastoral Writings*, all of my citations will be from this translation by Prof. Erik Hermann, Fortress Press, 2016). The Reformer takes up this challenge by directing his readers to Psalm 119 where he observes that David shows us how theologians are molded by prayer, meditation, and spiritual attack.

Luther maintains that he wishes to direct his readers to "a correct way of studying theology . . . taught by holy King David (and doubtlessly used also by the patriarchs and prophets) in the one hundredth nineteenth psalm. There you will find three rules, amply presented throughout the whole psalm. They are *oratio, meditatio, tentatio.*" According to Luther, these "rules" guide us in engaging the Holy Scriptures, the book that reigns supreme above all other writings for it alone teaches eternal life.

Genuine prayer (*oratio*) is created by God's Word. Before we can speak, we must listen. Prayer does not arise out of your own dark and desperate desires but out of God's command and promise. So David prays in Psalm 119, asking God to teach and tutor him:

"Blessed are you, O Lord; teach me your statutes!" (v. 12)

"When I told of my ways, you answered me; teach me your statutes" (v. 26).

"Teach me, O Lord, the ways of your statues; and I will keep it to the end" (v. 33).

"Lead me in the path of your commandments, for I delight in it" (v. 35).

"The earth, O Lord, is full of your steadfast love; teach me your statutes" (v. 64).

"You are good and do good; teach me your statutes!" (v. 68)

"Deal with your servant according to your steadfast love, and teach me your statutes" (v. 124).

"Make your face shine upon your servant, and teach me your statutes" (v. 135).

Luther observes that David wants us to "lay hold of the real teacher of the Scriptures himself [the Lord Jesus], so that he [David] may not seize upon them pell-mell with his own reason and become his own teacher." The apostle Paul says that pastors are to be apt to teach. The first step in becoming such a teacher is to be apt at learning. We learn from God's Word, imploring His Holy Spirit to teach us with and by the Word which He has inspired.

Next comes the *meditatio*. Meditation is not a turn toward inwardness and self-reflection. Rather it is reading and pondering the external words of the Holy Spirit as they come to us in the Holy Scriptures; it is taking them to heart and inwardly digesting them as one old prayer puts it. We meditate, that is, our hearts and minds are fixed on that in which we treasure and delight. Psalm 119 contains several images of this meditation on God's Word:

"Then I shall not be put to shame, having eyes fixed on all your commandments" (v. 6).

"I have stored up your word in my heart, that I might not sin against you" (v. 11).

"In the way of your testimonies I delight as much as in all riches" (v. 14).

"I will meditate on your precepts and fix my eyes on your ways. I will delight in your statutes; I will not forget your word" (vv. 15-16).

"Your testimonies are my delight; they are my counselors" (v. 24).

"Make me understand the way of your precepts, and I will meditate on your wondrous works" (v. 27).

"Turn my eyes from looking at worthless things; and give me life in your ways" (v. 37).

"For I find my delight in your commandments which I love. I will lift up my hands toward your commandments, which I love and I will meditate on your statues" (vv. 47-48).

"The law of your mouth is better to me than thousands of gold and silver pieces" (v. 72).

"How sweet are your words to my taste, sweeter than honey to my mouth!" (v. 103).

"Your word is a lamp to my feet and a light to my path" (v. 105).

"The unfolding of your words give light; it imparts understanding to the simple" (v. 130).

The Lutheran theologian, Oswald Bayer, notes, "It is true that Luther uses the word 'meditation' in an unusual way compared with the dominant usage of the received tradition. He actually gives it a meaning which no longer fully agrees with the traditional idea of meditation. In fact, Luther seems to all but reverse the normal meaning of the word, also in today's usage, when he focuses on the external word . . . Luther swims against the tide of common opinion in not seeing the process of listening turned inwards but rather opened outwards" (Oswald Bayer, *Theology the Lutheran Way*, Eerdmans, 2007). Mediation is verbal. It has to do with finding God where He has located Himself, namely, in His Word. Again, Bayer is very helpful here in reminding us, "Those who want to search for the Holy Spirit deep inside themselves, in a realm too deep for words to express, will find ghosts, not God."

Finally, there is *tentatio* or spiritual attack. The Christian life is an embattled life. You are a target for attack by God's enemies when you meditate on God's Word. Luther writes, "For as soon as God's Word takes root and grows in you, the devil will harry you, and make a real doctor of you, and by his assaults will teach you to seek and love God's Word." The life of David is the template for what you, too, will encounter. Psalm 119 records numerous confessions, supplications, and laments of David as he lived life under the cross of persecution from God's enemies:

"Even though princes sit plotting against me, your servant will meditate on your statues" (v. 23).

"The insolent smear me with lies, but with my whole heart I keep your precepts" (v. 69).

"It is good for me that I was afflicted, that I might learn your precepts" (v. 71).

"How long must your servant endure? When will you judge those who persecute me?" (v. 84)

"All your commandments are sure; they persecute me with falsehood; help me!" (v. 86)

"Depart from me, you evildoers, that I may keep the commandments of my God. Uphold me according to your promise, that I may live, and let me not be put to shame in my hope!" (vv. 115-116)

"Trouble and anguish have found me out, but your commandments are my delight" (v. 143).

"They draw near who persecute me with evil purpose; they are far from your law" (v. 150).

"Princes persecute me without cause, but my heart stands in awe of your words" (v. 161).

"Let my plea come before you; deliver me according to your word" (v. 170).

The *tentatio* that you will experience may come externally with persecution or it may come internally with doubts, struggle, and temptation. But these forces will drive you deeper into God's Word so that you meditate on Christ's promises and your lips will be unsealed to call upon His Name. In other words, Luther's triad works in reverse: The *tentatio* drives you back to the *meditatio*, and the *meditatio* to the *oratio*.

Prayer, meditation, and spiritual attack will shape your formation as a servant of God's Word. There is an abundance of resources that I could mention. For the time being, focus on the Holy Scriptures (especially the Psalms), the *Small Catechism*, and the hymnal. The Prayer Offices of the church like Matins and Vespers, the prayers of the Divine Service, and the hymns can be good tools in your personal prayers as well. Remember also that the *Small Catechism* is not only a book of doctrine but also a prayer book. For assistance in learning how to pray the catechism, you might look at my book, *Praying Luther's Small Catechism*.

God bless your preparation for the Office of the Holy Ministry by faithful study and prayer. In this way, the Triune God is shaping and forming you to be a servant in the image of Christ who will care for His flock with grace and truth.

Letter 11 – Office of the Holy Ministry

Rev. Kyle Krueger

So, you think you might want to be a pastor. Good. I think you should seriously consider it. Here's my one word of advice if you do, just don't be as bad as Jonah! But even if you are, God will still accomplish His will and have His Word proclaimed despite you. The Scriptures do NOT say, "for [the pastor] is living and active, sharper than any two-edged sword, piercing to the division of soul and of spirit, of joints and of marrow, and discerning the thoughts and intentions of the heart" (Hebrews 4:12). Rather, "the Word of God is living and active, sharper than any two-edge sword." Yes, it takes a preacher to preach God's Word, but as Jonah teaches us, God can even use a reluctant, self-centered preacher to bring many to repentance and faith. This is not because of who the preacher is, but because of who God is. So, let's explore some of Jonah's blunders and use them to encourage you toward the pastoral office.

Right off the bat in the Book of Jonah, God tells the prophet Jonah, a prophet being one who speaks God's Word, to "call out" (Jonah 1:2) against Nineveh. The Lord asks Jonah to do his job! Be a prophet. Be a preacher. Instead, Jonah gets up and tries to flee from God. Seriously, how pathetic of a prophet do you have to be to think you can escape from God? So, he hops a boat and tries to get as far away from God and Nineveh as he possibly can. He defies the Lord and refuses to do his job as a prophet to preach God's Word to the Ninevites. Despite his wrong direction, the Lord's Word will be spoken through him, and the pagan sailors on Jonah's getaway vehicle will turn to the Lord in repentance and faith.

Jonah gives the worst and most unconvincing witness ever to the pagan sailors: "And [Jonah] said to them, 'I am a Hebrew, and I fear the LORD, the God of heaven, who made the sea and the dry land.' Then the men were exceedingly afraid and said to him, 'What is this that you have done!' For the men knew that he was fleeing from the presence of the LORD, because he had told them" (Jonah 1:9-10). Here is a golden "evangelism" opportunity. Yet, Jonah tells them about how he, a prophet, is fleeing from the God he's supposed to prophesy for! Against all the odds, the Lord's Word was spoken to these pagan sailors and in the end, "the men feared the LORD exceedingly, and they offered a sacrifice to the LORD and made vows" (Jonah 1:16).

This is very good news for all considering the preaching office. Despite yourself, your sins, your screw-ups, your reluctance, your poor witness, the Lord will still use you to bring His Word of repentance and faith to whom He wills. Now, I certainly don't recommend you go out of your way to be like Jonah but let the Lord's success through Jonah's failures have you put your hope in the Lord and the power of His Word and not yourself or your skills or your personality. Jonah was simply the Lord's vessel. As a pastor you, too, would simply be the Lord's instrument.

Now the next encouraging example from Jonah for you to pursue the Holy Ministry is a bit more subtle, but of the utmost importance. As you well know, the Lord appoints a great fish to swallow Jonah. As the Lord is redirecting Jonah and calling him to repentance, Jonah proves himself to be both sinner and saint. So far in the narrative, Jonah shows much disdain toward the Lord, but in his prayer from the belly of the fish, we begin to see his faith. The content of Jonah's prayer is good and godly. Despite his dire and deathly situation, Jonah believes that the Lord can and will save him: "Then I said, 'I am driven away from your sight; yet I shall again look upon your holy temple.' [And,] I went down to the land whose bars closed upon me forever; yet you brought up my life from the pit, O LORD my God" (Jonah 2:4,6).

Jonah realizes that he cannot save himself. Only God can rescue him from his sinking, sinful situation. And this realization comes to a head with the final words of Jonah's prayer, "Salvation belongs to the LORD!" (Jonah 2:9) Of all the things Jonah gets wrong, this he gets right. He confesses that salvation is the Lord's and therefore it's His alone to give. As a pastor you will get a ton of stuff wrong! But keep this confession clear that salvation is the Lord's. It belongs to Him and Him alone. He won it and He grants it. And He will give it through weak and sinful pastors. If the worst preacher ever can do it, so can you. Despite yourself you are justified by grace for Christ's sake through faith. In other words, "Salvation belongs to the LORD!" And as He delivered Jonah from his downward, deathward spiral into the depths, He has delivered you from the depths of sin, death, and hell itself!

And finally, let's get to the heart of the matter in the Book of Jonah. In spite of all of Jonah's foolishness, the Lord ultimately brings him to the city of Nineveh. After all that Jonah had learned and experienced along the way, you would think he would muster up a sermon that would rival Peter's at Pentecost. After all he had seen the Lord do, after the great salvation Jonah had received from the deathly digestive juices of the fish, you would think this would be one epic sermon! Nope, not even close. Jonah calls out, "Yet forty days, and Nineveh shall be overthrown!" (Jonah 3:4) That's it. Pretty much the worst sermon ever. But despite the preacher, God's Word did its work. And it didn't take long. The very next verse tells us, "And the people of Nineveh believed God. They called for a fast and put on sackcloth, from the greatest of them to the least of them" (Jonah 3:5). The sermon was short, uninspiring, and lackluster, but God's Word through the worst preacher ever brings about mass repentance and faith!

At the end of chapter 3 we hear, "When God saw what they did, how they turned from their evil way, God relented of the disaster that he had said he would do to them, and he did not do it" (Jonah 3:10). God's Word was preached and immediately God granted repentance and faith to the evil Ninevites. From all outward appearances, Jonah was the wrong guy to do this, yet the Lord worked through him anyway. The God of all grace used a sinner to bring His Word to sinners. And miraculously it worked! The Lord has not stopped using Jonahs to proclaim His Word of salvation to the world.

And irony of ironies, Jonah's preaching endures today through the very mouth of Christ, the Word made flesh! The worst preacher ever is still preaching to this very day! Jesus Himself makes sinful Jonah useful again. Jesus proclaims His own saving death and burial using Jonah's struggle, "For just as Jonah was three days and three nights in the belly of the great fish, so will the Son of Man be three days and three nights in the heart of the earth. The men of Nineveh will rise up at the judgment with this generation and condemn it, for they repented at the preaching of Jonah, and behold, something greater than Jonah is here" (Matthew 12:40-41). Jonah becomes central to the proclamation of Christ crucified and risen! All this from a prophet who didn't want to speak God's Word and hopped a boat out of town to run from God!

Everything that happens in and through the prophet Jonah is a God-given miracle. If the Lord calls you to serve His Church as a pastor, everything you do and accomplish for the sake of the Gospel is also a God-given miracle. Despite yourself, people will hear God's Law and Gospel. They will be called to repentance and faith in Christ. As a preacher of God's Word, it's not about who you are, but about who the Lord is, the Bringer of eternal salvation to sinners.

Letter 12 – Psalms as Prayer Book

Rev. David Vandercook

Prayer is important, to say the least, for the pastoral ministry. It is part of the ordination vows that we take. The pastor-elect is asked if he will "be in constant prayer for those under [his] constant care." This takes on many different forms. There is the time spent in the study praying for your people on your own. There are the prayers that are offered in the sanctuary each week for those who are in need in your parish. Those times of prayer are perhaps a little bit easier, though, than the times spent in prayer at the parishioner's bedside, kitchen table, or living room. There are times of joy such as birthday and anniversary celebrations. There are times of sorrow such as sudden or prolonged illness, depression, end-of-life decisions, or comforting the bereaved. If you're anything like me, you might struggle to find the right words to say in a particular situation.

Pastors certainly are counted upon to say just the right thing at just the right time. Thankfully, we have the promise, as Paul writes, that "the Spirit helps us in our weakness. For we do not know what to pray for as we ought, but the Spirit Himself intercedes for us with groanings too deep for words" (Romans 8:26).

But what does that mean, exactly? I have encountered some who think this means that literally when you open your mouth, the right words will magically come out. That's a nice idea, but we know better than that. As the author of Hebrews writes: "Long ago, at many times and in many ways, God spoke to our fathers by the prophets, but in these last days He has spoken to us by His Son" (Hebrews 1:1-2a). The "many and various ways" that God used to communicate with the prophets consisted of direct revelation that took many different forms. In some cases, it was literally direct communication between God and His prophet. We see this in the way that Moses spoke with God. Sometimes it was through visions or dreams. That was "long ago," though. That was during the age of the prophets before the Incarnation. Now that Christ has come, God speaks to us differently. He speaks to us through His Word. In fact, as Luther writes, "[W]e must firmly hold that God grants His Spirit or grace to no one, except through or with the preceding outward Word, in order that we may [thus] be protected against the enthusiasts, i.e., spirits who boast that they have the Spirit without and before the Word, and accordingly judge Scripture or the spoken Word, and explain and stretch it at their pleasure . . ." *(Smalcald Articles* III, VIII, 3)

Now that we've determined that Paul was not a mystic, we still have the matter of what he was saying to the Romans. He was pointing out that as the baptized we have the Gift of the Holy Spirit. The Holy Spirit sanctifies us, that is, makes us holy. He even takes our muddled thoughts and words and presents them to our Father in heaven as if they weren't muddled at all.

This is no excuse for laziness, though. The fact is that not only does the Holy Spirit fix our prayers when they're lacking, but He also gives us an entire book of prayers to use. I'm talking about the Psalms. Right there in the middle of your Bible are 150 prayers. These prayers were written over hundreds of years by God's people who found themselves in pretty much any situation you can imagine. While they may have been written with a specific situation in mind, they've been written down for us and given to us to use when we find ourselves in similar situations.

Take, for example, Psalm 16. This psalm was written by David during what appears to have been a time of suffering for him. David cries out to God:

"Preserve me, O God, for in you I take refuge.
I say to the Lord, 'You are my Lord;
I have no good apart from you.'
The Lord is my chosen portion and my cup;
you hold my lot.
I have set the Lord always before me;

because he is at my right hand, I shall not be shaken.
Therefore my heart is glad, and my whole being rejoices;
my flesh also dwells secure.
For you will not abandon my soul to Sheol,
or let your holy one see corruption.
You make known to me the path of life;
in your presence there is fullness of joy;
at your right hand are pleasures forevermore" (Psalm 16:1-2, 5, 8-11).

As David suffers, he knows that the only true refuge that he can find is in God alone. He knows that there is no good apart from Him. Psalm 16 provides a fantastic prayer for anyone who is suffering. In particular, whoever is suffering physically can find comfort in these verses that remind them that God will never abandon them. David's firm faith in the face of suffering encourages those for whom we care to cling tightly to God's promises as well.

Jesus quoted the Book of Psalms more than any other book of the Scriptures. From the Cross, He prayed, "My God, my God, why have you forsaken me?" (Psalm 22:1a) Another psalm of David, Psalm 22, speaks from a place of deep sorrow and distress. Those whom we serve may feel that God has abandoned them. This psalm provides a prayer for the people of God in these seemingly hopeless situations. It is important to note that this psalm, even with its dark tone at the beginning, does remind those praying it that God has not abandoned them. Later on in the psalm, David writes:

"For he has not despised or abhorred
the affliction of the afflicted,
and he has not hidden his face from him,
but has heard, when he cried to him" (Psalm 22:24).

Not all ministry is done with those who are sick, suffering, or in despair. There are also times of celebration for which pastors are called upon to pray. Again, the psalms are more than adequate to give us the words to pray. The inscription for Psalm 30 indicates that David wrote it for the dedication of the temple. Of course, the temple wouldn't be built until after David's death, so it's possible that David wrote it knowing that it could or would be used for that purpose one day. Nonetheless, the psalm serves well as one of thanksgiving:

> "O Lord my God, I cried to you for help,
> and you have healed me.
> Sing praises to the Lord, O you his saints,
> and give thanks to his holy name.
> For his anger is but for a moment,
> and his favor is for a lifetime.
> Weeping may tarry for the night,
> but joy comes with the morning.
> You have turned for me my mourning into dancing;
> you have loosed my sackcloth
> and clothed me with gladness,
> that my glory may sing your praise and not be silent.
> O Lord my God, I will give thanks to you forever!"
> (Psalm 30:2, 4-5, 11-12)

This psalm could apply to a variety of occasions for giving thanks but seems particularly appropriate when one who was ill received healing from the Lord. It clearly acknowledges that God is the one who granted the healing. It also reminds us that the Lord chiefly desires to show mercy.

David, of course, didn't write all of the Psalms. Solomon, his son, the one who actually did oversee the building of the temple, wrote some as well. One of them, Psalm 127, speaks clearly of the blessings of marriage and family:

> "Unless the Lord builds the house,
> those who build it labor in vain.
> Behold, children are a heritage from the Lord,
> the fruit of the womb a reward.
> Like arrows in the hand of a warrior
> are the children of one's youth.
> Blessed is the man
> who fills his quiver with them!
> He shall not be put to shame
> when he speaks with his enemies in the gate" (Psalm 127:1, 3-5).

What a wonderful psalm that serves well on the occasion of a wedding or a wedding anniversary! It speaks of the importance of having the Lord at the center of marriage and also clearly acknowledges children as one of the chief blessings of marriage.

These are just a few examples of the beautiful prayers that God has given you in the Psalter to use in praying with those entrusted to your care or to use for yourself in preparing to serve those to whom you minister. You will almost certainly be troubled at times to find the right words to pray. Thanks be to God that the Book of Psalms gives you the words to pray and can shape the form of your entire prayer life.

Letter 13 – Holy Baptism

Rev. Anthony Oliphant

Pastors get interesting perspectives. I'm not just talking about theological perspectives—that's a given when you spend so much time in the Scriptures. Your take on the world and everyday matters is going to be shaped by that and you'll discover that your perspective will be quite different from a world that doesn't know God's Word. But I'm not talking about that. What I'm talking about are literal points of view. Pastors get to see the world from a different place than most, and it usually makes for an interesting experience.

For instance, one of my favorite views is of my congregation on Christmas Eve. Like many Lutheran congregations, we have a candlelight service. At the end of the service, we dim the sanctuary lights as we sing "Silent Night" by the light of all the candles held by those in the pew. From the chancel, in the front, I can see it all: every single candle, every face softly illumined by the glowing golden light, the entire sanctuary glowing as God's people sing about the birth of their Lord. It gives me a different perspective of Christmas Eve and our service that night.

But it's not only at special once-a-year services that I get to see things from a different angle. I get to experience a different view every single week. As the pastor at the front of the church, I get a unique perspective. I can connect dots in my line of sight that I wouldn't have if I were standing somewhere else. The most important of these dots is found at the baptismal font, which is just below the steps leading up to the altar. I stand there each week at the beginning of the service.

I intentionally stand in various places throughout the service. For prayers I stand in front of the altar, facing it, as a visual cue that I'm leading the congregation in prayer to God. When I read from God's Word I stand in the lectern and pulpit, showing that I'm not just giving my own ideas, but I'm speaking from an office, from a station wherein I'm under orders from the Lord to preach His Word of Law and Gospel. So, likewise, for confession and Absolution at the beginning of each service, I stand directly in front of the baptismal font. Why? So that when people look at me as I'm forgiving their sins, they connect that forgiveness with their Baptism; they see forgiveness flowing from the font. So many members of my congregation have been baptized in that very font. So many have been welcomed into God's holy ark, the Church, right there. So many have been given the Gift of faith and forgiveness, poured out on them through water and Word, in that exact spot. So, when I stand there and forgive sins as a called and ordained servant of the Word, I'm connecting each believer to his or her Baptism, whether I was the pastor who baptized them, or if it was one of my predecessors. From my vantage point, I get to collapse past, present, and future into that single eternal moment of the Gospel—their Baptism from before, the Absolution at that present moment, and the future proclamation they will hear at the end of time, when Christ returns and welcomes them into His eternal kingdom. Standing in that spot lets me see all that wrapped together in the grace of God on baptized believers.

The pastor's unique perspective continues. Confirmations are always a joyous occasion, with friends and family gathered in the pews to celebrate along with our confirmands. But from the chancel, being the one who puts my hands on their heads in blessing, seeing them kneel at the rail with the font behind them and their family and fellow believers all in the same line of sight—that's a view I wouldn't trade for anything. From my angle I get to see how the font is a physical, visual bridge between the confirmands and the wider Church. It's a visual token of what the Lord has done for all of them at their Baptism and what He's continuing to do. These confirmands are hearing the promises of Baptism echo in their ears again and the Church is celebrating with them. As the pastor who has taught these young people the Lord's Word, I get to see this connection—this ongoing fulfillment of God's promises to them—even if I wasn't the pastor who baptized them. From where I stand, I get to see a glimpse of a bigger picture of what Baptism is all about: being welcomed into the lasting promises of Jesus.

Those promises continue throughout the life of the baptized. There's another unique place I get to stand, but it's not for as joyful an occasion. At funerals, I'm in a place where others aren't. In fact, it's a place where many are uncomfortable. At the start of each funeral, I stand beside the casket, a universal symbol of death. But when I reach out my hand to touch the casket, I don't touch the cold material that will go in the ground. My hand is laid on the funeral pall, a beautifully made piece of fabric that's spread out and covers the entire casket, draping it in white and gold so that not a speck of that death symbol is visible. Death is swallowed up in the light of life. And where I stand, where the casket is placed, is directly in front of the baptismal font. The paschal candle is lit for the funeral service. The only other times we light it are for the season of Easter, celebrating when Jesus defeated death, and—you guessed it—when we have a Baptism. I have the honor of standing in the middle of all those symbols of life's victory over death, drawing them together to comfort the family and friends of the baptized who is now at peace. I get to remind the grieving of the promises God first made to them at the font, which He's now brought to fulfillment right there at the font again. My job—it's still a staggering thing to think about—is to weave those promises of life everlasting together into the beautiful picture of Christ's victory over the grave. My job is to preach life and salvation, to rejoice in the victory of the deceased that's theirs in Baptism, and to bring the comfort of Jesus' triumph to all those gathered.

And then, after the funeral, at the graveside, I tie all those promises together again. I stand at the yawning mouth of the grave. As the pastor, I lay my hand on the casket and say, "May God the Father, who created this body; may God the Son, who by His blood redeemed this body; may God the Holy Spirit, who by Holy Baptism sanctified this body to be His temple, keep these remains to the day of the resurrection of all flesh. Amen." Right there in the middle of the graveyard, death's domain, I throw Baptism into the face of death. Death cannot have this believer, this body, because the Holy Spirit has made this person His own temple. This Christian belongs to God, and on the Last Day this baptized body will rise again to live forever. From beginning to end, the promises at the font overflow into the life of Christians. And from where I stand it's a beautiful sight.

The things we do, the places we go, the words we use, the sights we see—these all shape us. Through Holy Baptism God shapes His people. Being the instrument God uses to bestow Baptism shapes the pastor. My sight is permeated with Baptism because I get to see it everywhere from where I stand, from the beginning of life in the Church to the very end; from the start of the service to the closing benediction; from Christmas Eve to every Sunday in the Church year. It's truly an honor being able to do that. It's my hope that in each sermon, in each pastoral encounter, I can relate what I see so that people would also see Baptism in every corner of their own lives. The grace of God is immense, and it changes the way we see things. It gives us a unique view, a new and beautiful perspective on everything.

Letter 14 – Lord's Supper

Rev. Dr. Matthew R. Richard

People seem to either be running from God or trying to find Him. You, as a future pastor, will do neither.

It is true that once you put on a clerical collar, every person that you meet in the marketplace will generally respond to you from one of those two groups. Even many of your future parishioners will oscillate back and forth between hiding from God and trying to climb into His good graces. That is to say, when people see your clerical collar, they will either sneer at you with awkward avoidance or draw near to you with giddy glee.

For those running from God, the reasons are quite complex. Maybe the Church has hurt them in the past. Or they see the clerical collar and feel unwanted guilt. Or they once tried to be spiritual, and it didn't work. Though this is not the case for every person, it has been my experience that many of these individuals run from God because they think God was not there for them when they needed Him the most. Furthermore, they despise the clerical collar because they perceive it as a symbol of an institution that does not give but rather takes. They run from God because, for them, God was not present. And the clergy, for them, are not servants but takers—demanding rules, money, and strict obedience to an unwritten churchly code of ethics.

For those trying to find God, their motives are a bit easier to understand. Generally speaking, they know they are sinners, feel guilt, and want to please God. But they do not know how. They see God as distant. They see Him as high and lofty. And they are doing their absolute best to bridge the gap between themselves and God. And so, every day, they are simply trying to be good enough to be in God's good graces. Like a neglected child trying to earn the approval of a busy father, these individuals have tender hearts filled with despair and uncertainty—always seeking, always trying, and always hoping to climb into the Lord's favor.

So, what does this have to do with you, dear future pastor? It is quite simple: Your task is neither to strategize with people to find God nor journey with people as they run away from God but rather to place the Lord into their hands, mouths, and bellies. You see, you are a servant of the Lord. And as His servant, you do not move away from the Lord or towards the Lord. You stand in your vocation as a pastor and deliver the Lord and His Gifts.

A close friend once told me a funny story. He said, "Imagine going to a party college. And at the front entrance there is a sign. And the sign says in bold capital letters, 'FREE BEER!'"

My friend went on to say, "After seeing a sign like this, the next great question would be, 'Where is the free beer?' Can you imagine the frantic emotions of the party students? Can you imagine the students saying, 'Where do we go? Will we get it? Is this a hoax? Is someone pulling our chain?'

Indeed, everyone would be in a frenzy, that is until someone would stand up and say, 'Everyone, listen up! Stop moving! Stop the frenzy! The free beer is right here!'"

As a future pastor, the point is quite clear! Your job is not to get sucked into the frenzy. Your job is not to give in to emotions, mystical endeavors, conjectures, or the like. Instead, you are to stand in your vocation as a pastor and boldly say, "Christ is right here. Free Gifts are right here, for you! Come and receive!"

Yes, your job is to deliver the Lord and His free Gifts. Your calling and vocation are to point to, speak about, and deliver that which is right before your people and those in the marketplace.

Sometimes pastors mess this up, though. Pastors of all denominations have said over the years, "Christ is right here," but, in reality, Christ is not found where they are pointing. In other words, pastors have pointed to the free Gifts of Christ in places where Christ has not promised to be. Alas, this only confuses things all the more! Pointing to Christ in all the wrong places will only make people seek even harder, or worse yet, give up altogether and abandon the faith.

You, dear future pastor, however, are being catechized in the one true faith. You are reading the Scriptures. You are hearing Christ's Word. You are hearing that Christ is present for you, and your future people, in the Word and Sacraments.

Imagine your future sanctuary for a moment. Think about the chancel area at the front of the church. This is where Christ has promised to be for you and your people. The font is where God snatches people from darkness unto light, marking them with His Triune Name. The lectern and pulpit are where Christ is really present, pouring His Word into open ears. And the altar is where beggars are invited to gather to receive, not free warm bread, but the very Body and Blood of Christ for the forgiveness of sins. Christ and His Gifts are received right there at the altar in the most Holy Supper.

Many people, though, will have a great deal of uncertainty with the Lord's Supper. Perhaps those who are running from God will say, "The Lord's Supper? I am too much of a sinner for such a holy meal. I must keep running; I am not worthy."

And those constantly trying to find the Lord may say, "I like communion; it is a kind of memorial where I must remember what He has done, and in so remembering Him, I might grasp Jesus more through my recollection."

Dear future pastor, again, you mustn't budge. You mustn't move. Do not flinch. Instead, you must declare that the people are not a part of some mere remembrance in the Lord's Supper, as though we kneel, eat, and imagine in our minds that we are memorializing a dead man. It is not a mental exercise to get closer to the Lord. Furthermore, you must declare that the Lord's Supper is a holy meal because it is a meal for sinners only, for sinners who need forgiveness. Sinners mustn't run from the table but be called to it!

You will find yourself in a most peculiar position at times. As people move around you, responding to the events of the world, your calling does not change. You do not move. You baptize. You preach. And you especially invite tired and restless souls to kneel at the communion rail because, right there at that rail and in the bread and wine, the Lord meets sinful humanity. At the rail, on one's knees, is right where that sinful mankind stops his running and seeking in order to receive forgiveness, life, and salvation. And you, dear future pastor, simply hand over the Gifts!

Never forget, regardless of the situation, context, or day, the Lord's Supper is present. His Gifts are unending. And you, dear future pastor, are the one who hands over the goods. You are the one who delivers. You invite people to the church, not to bolster attendance or increase monetary giving but instead, you invite everyone you encounter so that they might stop running and seeking. You invite them to the table, so that they can receive on their knees with open hands, mouths, and ears. How glorious: The Lord's Supper is a holy meal that brings the seeking, the wandering, the troubled, and the despairing together to receive assurance upon tongues and into bellies!

Do not run. Do not seek. Do not move, dear future pastor. Stand firm. Distribute God's Gifts. Deliver Christ. Invite people to kneel at the table to receive, and so, fulfill your vocation.

Letter 15 – Confession and Absolution

Rev. Duane Bamsch

In the 95 Theses, Martin Luther wrote, "When our Lord and Master Jesus Christ said, 'Repent' (Matthew 4:17), he willed the entire life of believers to be one of repentance." It was not without reason that Dr. Luther fired his "shot across the bow" against the Roman Church's troubling of consciences. He realized what the very point of contention in the Christian faith was: How is forgiveness given? Is forgiveness earned or is it freely given? He saw the tipping point between despair and peace on display in the callousness of the institutional Church toward those who struggled in their sin (and in those who were secure in their sin as well). It is not an easy task to preach Law and Gospel, to afflict the comfortable and to comfort the afflicted—and yet this is at the heart of everything that you as a pastor will be called to do.

The call to repentance can only be made to poor, miserable sinners if there is a remedy offered in response to that repentance. That remedy is the immeasurable mercy of God the Father given in Holy Absolution, the very forgiveness of all sin. And truly, Absolution isn't the response to repentance, but repentance is how the sinner responds to the offer of Absolution. More on that in a moment.

The Rite of Confession and Absolution is one of the most wonderful, yet terrifying, Gifts that the Lord of the Church places in the hands of His under-shepherds. This is why it stands between the Sacraments of Holy Baptism and the Lord's Supper in the catechisms. Holy words are spoken directly to troubled consciences in desperate need of succor. A Gift from the Lord is given that delivers forgiveness, life, and salvation.

On that first Easter evening it was the Risen Christ Himself, in glorified and resurrected flesh, who said to His terrified, locked-away disciples (and to you!): "If you forgive the sins of any, they are forgiven them; if you withhold forgiveness from any, it is withheld." What an awesome and weighty responsibility! You will hold, in the Holy Office bestowed upon you with the yoke of service, the forgive-ness (or the binding) of the sins of a sinner, depending on whether or not that one is truly penitent. And that binding or loosing has consequences reaching into eternity.

How does one deal with such a frightening responsibility?

This is the reason that Dr. Luther encourages in the *Large Catechism* that "when I urge you to go to confession, I am simply urg-ing you to be a Christian." He urges you to take advantage of the Gift you will give. Again, he sees the heart of the life of faith—submission before the God and Lord of heaven and earth, of all things visible and invisible. It is the recognition that we live and move and have our being only in the Living God.

All creation falls upon its knees in acknowledgment that, as the psalmists say (and Paul repeats), "None is righteous, no not one" (Romans 3:11). It is true that "all have sinned and fall short of the glory of God" (Romans 3:23). No one can stand before the Lord God on his own merits and claim a place. Sin indeed separates creation from the Creator for all eternity. The sinful turn away in fear, and the Holy God cannot behold such impurity.

This is the Law you will preach. These are the holy admoni-tions you must proclaim to those secure in their sin, not unlike the prophets of old who were given utterances to speak, whether or not their hearers listened. And there will be times when you will have the fears of Jeremiah, or the despair of Elijah. Like Ezekiel, you will feel like a clown, miming the things of the Lord while people look on in mockery. But each of these men, and every man called by the Lord of the Church throughout history, were charged with Holy Orders to speak what He had given them to proclaim.

It wasn't all doom and gloom, though. Isaiah reminded his fel-low believers tenderly, "Comfort, comfort my people, says your God." Micah promised One who would shepherd God's people into a place of peace and safety. Zechariah prophesied that our King was coming in victory, even though He would strangely enter that cosmic battle upon a donkey's colt. These promises then unfold in the Holy Gospels with the proclamations that the Son of God has become man for us and for our salvation. These proclamations lead the Christian to the Cross, perched upon the lonesome rock of Golgotha, where the Lord of Life gives His away in sacrifice for the life of the world.

It is that sacrifice—one for all people, once for all time—that opens the floodgates of righteousness for the Christian, for the sinner, for the despised, and for the rejected. For it is in that death and life of the Son of God that all sin is atoned for. It is in that sacrifice that all sin is forgiven. It is in that sacrifice that God and man are reconciled. This is the Gospel you will proclaim.

And this is why the repentance a sinner speaks is a response. It is not something "earned" by confessing. The "work" of forgiving has been done. The price has been paid, the debt has been canceled. Much like an unexpected package arriving at your door, the Gift is yours; your name is even on it! And it is a Gift of such extravagance and beauty, given in astounding love and mercy, that one can't even consider rejecting it unless one has a heart hardened by sin and hatred to the point that one sees oneself as the final arbiter of truth.

Seeing the depth of the riches and mercy of God given in the Gift of Absolution, the penitent can only respond as King David did: "I acknowledged my sin to you, and I did not cover my iniquity; I said, 'I will confess my transgressions to the LORD,' and you forgave the iniquity of my sin" (Psalm 32).

In your ordination, you will be charged to gladly hear the sins confessed to you, and also to never, ever divulge them. Never. That is the terrifying part; for you may never expect the depth and depravity of the sin that comes tumbling out of the mouth of the penitent one who deeply desires Absolution.

In some cases, you may consider the confessed sin to not be so serious, wondering why the one confessing to you is on the verge of collapse and afraid to speak from a shame felt deep within over this sin that he truly fears will separate him from God's grace and mercy for all of eternity.

Then again, the sinner may well confess something you know to be utterly horrific, yet it seems as though the words spoken haven't even caused the confessor to blink.

In the midst of these extremes, remember that these sinners aren't confessing their sins to you. They have trusted that it was Almighty God—Father, Son, and Holy Spirit—who baptized them and washed them and named them as His own. They have trusted that He is trustworthy and true when He says that any sin confided to Him is removed as far as the east is from west.

In their bones they need to hear that the same Lord who baptized them, who enlivened them with the Spirit, and who washed them clean with His blood, has taken this specific sin as well and removed it from them. That Jesus has taken that sin upon His shoulders, borne it with His Cross, died with it, and left it in His tomb on Easter morning.

In a very real sense, as you hear confession from the penitent sinner, you are forgiveness enfleshed. You are the "physical element" of the "sacrament" of confession and Absolution. Your very real voice speaks the words of God's Absolution: "In the stead and by the command of my Lord Jesus Christ I forgive you all your sins in the name of the Father and of the + Son and of the Holy Spirit."

When you place your hand on the forehead or drape your stole over the head of the penitent and ask if he believes "that [your] forgiveness is God's forgiveness," you drape the Lord's robe over him, the very hem the woman with the flow of blood reached for to bring healing.

In this binding and loosing of sins, you straddle the gulf between sin and holiness, death and life. You have been charged with applying the balm of forgiveness to the wounded and pricking the consciences of the comfortable.

Do not be afraid of this responsibility, my brother. It is indeed weighty and serious. But it is also the Lord's Gift, set aside for you to freely give to those in need. Receive it as freely as you give it, for Satan will try and distract and mislead you, but the promise of our triumphant Lord wins every time. Amen.

Letter 16 – Theology of History

Rev. Dr. James Ambrose Lee II

Within the parish and the classroom, I have encountered faithful and pious Christians who have questioned the importance of Church history. "Why," the Christian muses, "is it important that I study the history of the Church? Why can't I simply study the Bible?" To be sure, we must admit at the outset that the Bible is the inspired and inerrant Word of God, lacking nothing regarding the message of man's redemption in Jesus Christ. We don't need to add to it or expand it. That doesn't mean, however, that Church history is merely superfluous or ornamental to the Christian faith. In fact, a thorough knowledge of the history of Christ's Church reinforces and bolsters one's confession of the faith. It is essential for all Christians, but especially for pastors and those desirous of the Office of the Holy Ministry.

As members of Christ's one, holy, catholic, and apostolic Church, we take history seriously because we see this already reflected in God's own Word. Consider how God first reveals Himself when He speaks to Moses from the burning bush, "I am the God of your father, the God of Abraham, the God of Isaac, and the God of Jacob" (Exodus 3:6). God identifies Himself by reference to the history of Israel. To know the One speaking now, Moses must know Him through His historical words and works. God calls Moses to know Him in relation to the salvific acts and events that God brought about for the sake of the patriarchs. And so it was for the children of Israel after Moses and the Exodus. Israel was to understand her relationship to God by seeing it through the lens of Israel's own history with God, for example, as we read in Deuteronomy 32.

The Christian Church and her confession are not founded upon ahistorical myths ("A long time ago in a galaxy far, far away. . ."), or philosophical speculations, or pious platitudes. The Christian Church confesses her faith in the one, eternal, and infinite Triune God, who created time itself ("maker of heaven and earth"), who entered into human history, not randomly, but by joining human nature to Himself ("conceived by the Holy Spirit, born of the Virgin Mary"). In Jesus Christ, God became man; the infinite enters finitude; the eternal embraces history. Just as it was foreshadowed in Israel, the salvation of humanity, accomplished in and through Jesus, occurs in time, through historical acts (the life, death, resurrection, and ascension of Jesus, and the pouring out of the Holy Spirit) that define the Church's relationship with God.

The centrality of history for the Church does not terminate with the death of the apostles, or even after the composition of St. John's Revelation. From the Incarnation onward, the vision of the Christian Church is shaped by history. To be sure, the Christian Church does not believe in an ongoing revelation of truth, where God gradually reveals new truth to the Church. The fullness of God's revelation has been revealed in the Word made flesh and the divinely inspired Word of God. The Church's articulation of God's revelation of truth receives greater clarity as Christians reflect upon the biblical witness. In fact, often, it is through battling against error and false teaching that the Christian Church arrives at a more precise and clear articulation of the theological language that she uses to confess Christ and His teachings.

An example that illustrates this is the Nicene Creed. This creed is regularly recited by Christians as a trinitarian and Christological confession of the faith of the Church. When we recite this creed, we Christians confess that the Son of God is in fact God, equal to the Father with respect to His divinity. Although the theological basis of the Nicene Creed is Scripture, its specific theological articulation only arose in response to the teaching of the fourth-century Alexandrian presbyter, Arius, who taught that the Son of God is dissimilar to the Father, possessing an unequal relationship to the Father. In order to preserve the unique dignity of the Father, Arius proclaimed that Christ, the Son, although begotten before all things, and even the creator of all things, did not share the same essence with the Father.

The Council of Nicaea rejected Arius's Christology. The Council Fathers confessed the Son to be equal to the Father ("God of God, light of light, very God of very God"), to the extent that the Son is of the same substance with the Father. The doctrinal foundation of the Nicene Creed is taken from the Scriptures, but the creed itself is a direct response to heresy.

Or consider how Luther confesses the Lord's Supper in his *Small Catechism*. Luther's language is clear, drawn from Jesus' words in the Gospels and from Paul. Luther teaches with a biblical voice that is both simple and precise. Our appreciation of Luther's teaching only grows when we understand Luther's teaching within his historical context. The clarity with which Luther confesses the bodily presence of Christ in the Supper stands out in sharp contrast against reformers such as Zwingli, Oecolampadius, and Calvin, who rejected the bodily presence of Christ, making the Lord's Supper into either a memorial meal or into mere spiritual eating. In contrast, the Church of Rome had transformed the Lord's Supper into a sacrifice offered to God on behalf of the living and those in purgatory, Luther taught that the Sacrament of the Altar is the true Body and Blood of Jesus, given in bread and wine (not other elements), instituted by Christ Himself, for the forgiveness of sins, received through the eating and drinking of His Body and Blood in faith. Against the memorializing interpretation of the Reformed and the unbiblical errors of Rome, Luther proclaimed the words of Jesus and confessed the Sacrament as mandated by Christ Himself.

Neither the Council of Nicaea nor Luther were the recipients of new revelations from God. Nor did they envision themselves as creating new articles of faith for the Church. Yet, both the Council and Luther helped the Church articulate Her confession of faith with greater nuance and specificity. Ignorance of these historical developments does not mean that a person's faith is weak or in jeopardy. But a greater understanding and appreciation of the history of the Church creates a greater understanding of the Christian faith and her confession of Jesus Christ. Unlike the Mormons and some Christian confessions who reject post-biblical Christian history or consider it wholly tainted by error and apostasy, Lutherans rejoice in the history of the Church. Although we are not uncritical recipients of the past, we receive Christian history, and hold that it is pivotal in helping

shape our understanding of the Christian confession and our iden-
tity as fellow Christians. The study of Christian history brings us
and our day into conversation with the great Christian voices of the
past. Their writings, their voices, and their confession bolster our
voices and our confession. Like the patriarchs of Israel before, the
Christian Church sees the present from the perspective of the past.
We receive the benefit of our confession being shaped by the faithful
who confessed before us.

Letter 17 – Theology of Preaching

Rev. Chris Hull

David was a man after God's own heart as we read in 1 Samuel 13:14: "But now your kingdom shall not continue. The Lord has sought out a man after his own heart, and the Lord has commanded him to be prince over his people, because you [Saul] have not kept what the Lord commanded you." We remember reading of David's slaying Goliath and trusting in the Lord to protect him. We read of David's relying on God while Saul pursued him to kill him. We remember David's holiness and righteousness in various psalms where he was led along by the Holy Spirit to praise God for His mercy and love.

Lest we forget, David was also a great sinner. For as we read in 2 Samuel 11-12 we see a David not after God's heart and Word, but rather a man bent on fulfilling and satisfying the desires of his sinful heart. David coveted Uriah's wife, Bathsheba, then stole her by deceiving everyone around him. After fulfilling his adulterous lust, David butchered Uriah. From the beginning of this pursuit to the end, David broke every commandment of God and lived in smug hypocrisy. David lived in ignorance of his sins against God and his neighbor because he was consumed with lust for the things of this life. David would not come to the knowledge of his sins and therefore could not rest assured in the love of God.

But God did not leave David in this state. Rather, in merciful love, God sent the prophet Nathan to David. Nathan came to David and preached the Law to him with the story of the rich man and the poor man. The rich man had many sheep, while the poor man had one little ewe lamb. When the rich man had an honored guest, he stole the poor man's little lamb to feed his guests, even though he had many lambs of his own. Nathan told this story and then asked David what should happen to this man. David, in "righteous" anger, said that the rich man should be punished and put to death. Nathan then pointed the finger of the Law and said, "That's you, David. You are the man. You took your neighbor's wife and killed your neighbor to satisfy your fallen desires." David repented and was healed in the words of Holy Absolution spoken by God through the mouth of His servant Nathan. God did not let David abide in the ignorance of his sins and therefore be condemned in them. Instead, He sent Nathan to proclaim the Law and the Gospel so that David would be liberated and delivered from sin, death, world, and the power of the devil.

This is preaching, my brother. Every man, woman, and child is David. In sin did our mothers conceive us. We were brought into this world not with the image of righteousness imprinted on our hearts, but rather we were born concupiscent and inclined to fulfill in ignorant bliss the sinful desires of our corrupted hearts. There is not one man, except our Lord Jesus Christ, conceived and born without sin. There is no one who is righteous, no, not one. However, because man is thus corrupted, he will never come to acknowledge this depravity, in the same manner that David was ignorant. The Law must be preached for man to recognize his sin and know that he needs to be saved. The Law is preached to rebuke sin that man may know that he is not holy in himself. David believed himself holy until Nathan's lawful finger pointed at him, and David cried out, begging for mercy.

You will be sent one day into the lives of those you are called to serve to preach this very same Law. You will be called and placed into the Holy Office to preach the Law, that man may have a righteous despair and lament his sinful condition. You are sent to preach the Law that man may cry out along with Paul, "Wretched man that I am! Who will deliver me from this body of death?" (Romans 7:24)

You will preach the Law for this reason, that man may know his sin and put to death any notion of self-righteousness. However, watch, lest you preach the Law without the Gospel. As the *Lutheran Confessions* teach us, "The mere use of the law without Christ either produces presumptuous people, who believe that they can fulfill the law by external works, or drives man utterly to despair" (*Formula of*

Concord-Solid Declaration v.10, Tappert). You may one day become the greatest preacher of the Law, making the repentance preaching of John the Baptist superfluous. However, if you do not at the same time preach the Gospel with equal fervor and clarity, then you will either create self-righteous Pharisees who never need Christ, or consciences so terrified that they will never believe they can be loved by God. It is a blessing to be able to preach the Law with clarity. However, it is an even greater blessing to know when the Law has done its work in order that the Gospel may enter into the sinful soul to quicken it.

Remember, brother, that when David repented, Nathan was quick to proclaim the Holy Absolution. May this be the same for you in preaching the Gospel to those timid souls crushed by the Law. Be quick to preach the Cross of Jesus for the conscience-stricken. Think on it this way: You are never going to convert the Pharisee by preaching more Law, but you will leave the terrified without any hope when you do so. Forget trying to convert the Pharisee with the Law, and instead turn your heart and mouth to the terrified and pour into them the love of God that is theirs in Christ Jesus their Lord. Pour into them the mercy that is theirs in the forgiveness that Jesus purchased and won on the Cross for them. For that is why you are there. You are called and placed there to hand over the Gifts of the Cross, to distribute the benefits of forgiveness, life, and salvation that Jesus won on the cursed tree almost 2,000 years ago. The terrified cannot go back in time to the Cross. Therefore, Jesus has sent you to bring the Good News of the Cross to them in the forgiveness of their sins.

This, my brother, is the theology of preaching. You preach the Law and rightly distinguish it from the Gospel so that you may save that trapped sinner in the proclamation of Holy Absolution. You are placed there to preach into their ears the saving Word of the Cross, that there is not one sin that Jesus did not die on the Cross for. Yes, I know that is bad grammar, but it gets the point across. There isn't anything left to condemn that saint. All in Jesus is forgiven. Jesus claimed all their sins, wrapped Himself up completely in their transgressions, in order that they may be wrapped up in the forgiving words of the Gospel and covered in the righteousness of Christ that covers all their sins. Jesus calls and places you to cover the sinner up in His righteousness so that the Father may see only the saint. You are sent with the Good News of the Gospel to reckon sinners to be saints in the forgiveness of their sins. You are sent forth to heal every saint and bind up their wounds in the blood, wounds, and death of Jesus.

I leave you with this comfort: The day that Jesus ordains you and places you in a congregation, He promises to never leave you nor forsake you. When you preach, you are not alone. You have the Word of God as your voice and your Lord Jesus as your strength. Jesus stands behind you and encourages you as you grant immortality in the forgiveness of all the sins of your hearers. Jesus goes before you, showing you where to speak and when to stop speaking. Jesus gives you the words to say in His Holy Word so that you may never be caught off guard. Jesus desires you to be His man in that time and place to comfort the terrified conscience and speak peace into every troubled heart. Know that the devil hates your guts for wanting to be a pastor and a preacher. He hates it when you preach the Law as it is given, and the Gospel as it is needed. He despises that you liberate timid souls from their fear of death and God's wrath against their sin.

The devil may have nothing but disdain for you, but Jesus smiles with delight because you are doing the good work of rightly dividing the Word of Truth so that the souls entrusted to you may be freed from the fear of their enemies. So, just preach, and let God worry about everything else. Preach until you lose your voice. Preach so that the terrified may know that God loves them. "Preach you the Word, and plant it home And never faint; the Harvest Lord Who gave the sower seed to sow will watch and tend His planted Word" ("Preach You the Word" LSB 586, st.6).

Letter 18 – Theology of Ethics

Rev. Dr. Scott Stiegemeyer

As you consider pastoral ministry, it's important to understand that sometimes people make a distinction between morality and ethics and give them different definitions. But for the purpose of this letter, I'll use the terms interchangeably. So, if you're not too familiar with the term "ethics," just think of "Christian moral teaching." This article is about holy living, but before we can say what it is, we have to say what it is not.

First of all, ethics is not the central focus of God's Word. The Bible is not about how to be more obedient and submissive to the Law. Some people imply, or even explicitly say, that your own personal holiness is the primary message of Christianity. But that is not true.

The central message of the Bible is Jesus Christ, the Savior of the world. And the doctrine of how sinners are justified is at the heart of our message. The basis of justification is the Cross. We believe and proclaim that human beings are brought into a right relationship with God by Jesus' death for the forgiveness of our sins. God credits our sinfulness to His Son on the Cross and credits the innocence and righteousness of Jesus to us. That is the Good News! Believe it. We contribute nothing to our justification except our sins which are taken away by Jesus Christ.

God credits the holiness of Jesus to you. That's salvation. God also makes you holy yourself, conforming you to the image of His Son (Romans 8:29). That is called sanctification. One of the fundamental documents explaining Lutheran doctrine is called the *Augsburg Confession*. About sanctification, it says, "Faith should yield good fruit and good works ... but [we should] not place trust in them as if thereby to earn grace before God." So, walking according to God's commandments is the result (fruit) of justification, not the cause of it. And even that is empowered by Christ living in you.

Many of the moral questions we face are clearly addressed in Holy Scripture. An obvious example would be sex outside of marriage. Sexual desire, itself, is not necessarily the problem. God has created human beings to form a life-long faithful union with a member of the opposite sex. That does not mean that everyone must get married, of course. Some people never marry for reasons they don't control, and they are no less God's magnificent creations. And God has gifted some individuals with the ability to remain single for the purpose of serving the His kingdom, but that is rare. Most people will marry. Desiring intimacy, companionship, and union with a woman if you are a man and a man if you are a woman is natural and good. The problem is that original sin has so polluted our hearts that now we are tempted to relate sexually to people in ways that are not according to God's plan (homosexual activity, pornography, adultery, etc.).

When the Bible is explicit, the options are clear. However, there are other things that God's Word speaks to but which it might not address explicitly. Human beings sometimes need to use our God-given reason, always submitting to Scripture, to work out the best solutions. We call this ethics. The Christian mind, which has been shaped and informed by the truths of Scripture, will approach ethics differently from the non-Christian.

Some ethicists try to develop foundational principles to help us make the tough moral decisions. One of those principles is called "utilitarianism." When stuck with an ethical dilemma, utilitarians try to figure out which actions will cause the most happiness and the least sadness. Is this a good guiding moral principle for Christians at those times when Scripture is not explicit? It certainly sounds good, and you can imagine situations when that may be fine. But it is a bad foundation for morality in general. For example, let's say there is a homeless man lying unconscious in a hospital emergency room. No one knows who he is. And now let's say that there are five dying patients in the same hospital who desperately need organ transplants to survive. One needs a heart, two others need a single lung each, and two more need a kidney. There's this homeless man with healthy organs which happen to match the needs of the dying patients. Someone suggests killing the homeless man to harvest his organs to save the other five people. Why not? No one will miss him. And it's one life to save five. Hypothetically, in this little thought experiment, a utilitarian could say, "Do whatever causes the most happiness and the least unhappiness. Yes, one dies, but five more survive."

Christian ethicists would completely oppose this move. We may never directly kill an innocent person, no matter who he is, even to save someone else (or five). Every single human life is precious, made in the image of God, and redeemed by the sufferings of Jesus. Apply this to the destruction of human children in embryonic form. Directly killing them is wrong, even if the intention is to perform experiments which might save more lives later.

"But what about personal freedom and choice?" someone will ask. "Sure," they might say, "there are some limits, but shouldn't I be allowed to decide for myself when and how to have sex? Or to marry anyone of whatever sex? Or whether to have an abortion?" This idolization of personal liberty is common, but it is contrary to Christianity.

We do have extraordinary freedom to live in the world within the limits of what a human being is meant to be. Christians are not determinists. That is, we don't believe that you are predetermined by the stars, your genes, or God to go to a certain school, to take a certain job, or marry a certain person. And certainly, as Christians we have freedom from the threat of God's Law. The righteousness to stand before God is a Gift. That's very freeing.

But freedom never means that you can do or be anything you want. One way to think about this is to consider what it means to be a human being. We have a human nature that identifies what we truly are and what our purpose is. Here is an illustration. An apple tree that is true to its nature and purpose will be beautiful, bear delicious fruit, provide branches for firewood, and give shade from the blazing sun to those beneath its branches. For an apple tree to be able to live and grow according to how God has created it is magnificent and beautiful. But if that apple tree could choose not to bear fruit, or to attempt to bear tomatoes instead of apples, or to only shade people it likes, then it would be a mess. It would fail as an apple tree. That's because it's not living according to its God-given nature or purpose.

Humans are like that. We have a human nature, a way to exist and live that our Father intends. When we try to live in ways that go against our God-given nature or purpose, though, we don't find ourselves. We don't experience freedom. We don't live the good life. We get only the opposites of those things: We become lost, experience slavery, and lose our lives. Tragically, our human nature is now corrupted by sinfulness and our purpose is obscured. We are spiritually blind, dead, and enemies of God.

Every sin starts out as unbelief. The devil tempts us to sin with promises of liberty and life. But he's a liar and the father of lies. He always promises more and delivers less. He wants you to doubt God, to lose faith, to think that God doesn't really have your best interests at heart. Under the devil's deception, we stop seeing God as our Father and our truest friend, and instead see Him as our adversary. We start to feel that God is withholding something that we ought to have. We think that we can get something good without God that we can't get with Him. And thus, we oppose Him. Things can't get more backwards than that. Since the Fall into sin, we are not in our right minds. We can't see things as they really are. And we cannot lift ourselves out of this pit.

Thanks be to God, we are not left to rot in our misery. Jesus, the Savior, pays the price for our guilt. His blood ransoms us from bondage to death. He rose from the dead and now shares that same victory with those who are baptized into Him. Jesus is our freedom. He is our wisdom, righteousness and sanctification and redemption (1 Corinthians 1:30). We may get bogged down with life's questions, sin, and feel like failures as far as holy living. But that is not the last word. We share grace with people who fall short, including ourselves. With repentance and Absolution comes restoration from the Lord. United to Christ in Baptism, the life you live is Christ living in you (Galatians 2:20). This Gospel truth is what will drive you in all of your vocations, whether or not you are ultimately called to be a pastor.

Letter 19 – Justification and Sanctification

Rev. Harrison Goodman

Let's start with a few brief definitions:

Justification: God's work of saving sinners through the death and resurrection of His Son, not according to our works, but wholly by grace received by faith.

You can find words like "just" and "justice" in there. You are declared innocent. Jesus was punished for your sin. It is finished. Full stop.

Sanctification: God's work of making the sinner holy by the working of the Holy Spirit through the Word and Sacraments.

You can find words like "saint" and the "Sanctus" in there. It means holy. Sanctification is your being made holy by God. Every day the Old Adam is drowned. Every day the New Man arises to live before God in righteousness and purity forever. It's still going on. Christians must do good works.

Frustration: being told you're holy and falling back into sin over and over again. Struggling against the flesh and marking God's promises in yourself rather than in His Word.

The life of the Christian is lived at the intersection of justification and sanctification. It's maddening. One of my professors told us the great error is asking, "Did it work?" rather than, "Is it true?" God calls us to do good works. He promises we're holy. We preach to sinners who lose more than they win. Our daily struggles against the flesh don't leave much to hope for. Left alone with Old Adam, justification and sanctification turn into doubt and despair.

Doubt. Despair. Were words like these created by God? Did they exist before the Fall? They don't seem like they fit into a creation which the Book insisted was good. Did we invent them? Were words like "doubt" and "despair" hidden seeds inside of poisoned fruit stolen from the garden of the Divine? Luther said the Tree of Knowledge of Good and Evil was the first church. It was a good tree, given that we would see that there's something bigger than ourselves in a universe that seems so vast and yet mundane at the same time. There was a God who knew awful words like "evil" and hid them in fruit so we'd never have to find them. There was a God who understood the things we wish we could. And more, there was a God who, from before the foundation of the world, sought only to cover words like "despair" in blood-soaked hope. The same Book says the Lamb was slain before the foundation of the world. If words like "doubt" and "despair" were seeds of the fruit of the first church, those words shouldn't be so hard to utter in ours.

The Church was given to contain all the doubt and despair. To confront the intersection between God's declaration that you are holy, His promising to make you holy, and your inability to demonstrate it. It was given to cover wretched words with hope. The fruit looked good, even though it contained so much evil. God said it actually was good. Maybe the fruit of the Tree of Knowledge of Good and Evil was never a trap, but a promise. God covers doubt, despair, and all that is evil and profane with a promise we behold in awe-struck hope. God can cover our evil in beauty. In good. In blood. The tree was good, given to find peace, not to play pretend. Not play God.

This is still what we do in church. We play God. We play the righteous. We dress up as the ones who build the kingdom, containing only what's pure. We pretend we fulfill those Ten thou-shalt-nots. We pretend to be as good as the Law demands. We pretend the Law describes us, and not the God who created it. We pretend to be the ones who are here to help God, and not the ones full of poisoned seed, passed down from the very first one. But what if it's the same? God's Tree of Knowledge of Good and Evil, the first church, was full of fruit filled with evil that He'll cover with a promise and then use for good. What if those wretched things inside us don't stop us from being worthy of love? What if they're the very things that make us belong? We're the sinners who need Jesus. The justified and the being sanctified. The Church is built on the Gospel, not the Law. It's built on the Christ, and not the Christian. It's built on the promise of blood spilled to cover sin and guilt and shame and it rests on an empty tomb that sings hope to every jilted whispered doubt.

God was upfront about what was in the fruit of the first church. There's bad stuff in there. Maybe we shouldn't be so afraid to admit the same. I'm filled with doubt. I'm filled with despair. And I'm hanged with Christ on the tree of death, united to Him in Baptism so that I would be united with Him in the Tree of Life, too.

Justification and sanctification appear to exist in tension. It's not because one comes from God and the other comes from us; both are the work of God. It's because one is finished now, and the other, not yet. The tension is a question of time, not you. We live shy of the resurrection. Until then, you do not do the good you want, but the evil you do not want is what you keep on doing. Sin dwells within you. Death dwells within you, but life, too, in Christ.

That's not something to despair over. The tension is the thing that brings joy. It gives comfort in our failure. It gives hope to our struggle. The tension between justification and sanctification means you have permission to use what's promised to you. Mercy. Forgiveness. You have permission to struggle, to fail, to doubt. None of those are good things, but none of them can overcome the promise God makes to sinners. That's why the devil would have you focus on yourself and not on what's done. It's why he'd ask, "Is it working?" which points to the death in you, and not, "Is it true?" which is only measured in the resurrection of Jesus. Satan turns good works into a chance to prove something, not a chance to help in love the guy next to you who is struggling with the same thing.

It's why I hate that awful poem about footprints. It isn't just because it boasts that we walk with God more than He drags us kicking and screaming. It isn't even that the whole thing is painted on a white, sandy beach instead of the valley of the shadow of death. It's that there are only two sets of footprints. There are a lot of us down here, all being dragged through the valley. What's utterly miraculous is that He uses us to drag each other. We stagger along, surrounded by so great a cloud of witnesses. Let us also lay aside every weight and sin which cling so closely. Those belong to Jesus now. Let us limp with endurance the race that is set before us. But let us do it together. We are the Body of Christ, knit together under Him who is the Head.

I think the race isn't our personal journey of self-discovery and self-improvement. I think it's the life of the one holy Christian and apostolic Church. It's the baton passed from John to Polycarp to Irenaeus to generation upon generation and then to you. It's a bloody race full of martyrs. With their dying last steps, they cried, "Christ is risen." Because His death and resurrection change everything. And they change nothing at all. We run the same race as those gone before us. You have their same fears. Their same sins. Their same doubts. Their same failures. And you have their same Jesus. The race, the path, the way we stagger along is the way of holiness. Even if they are fools, they shall not go astray.

I'm still afraid they'll find out what a sinner I am. How much cowardice hides behind bold words preached to desperate ears! I must still be here because we're the only thing the tree can be filled with. We're sin-wrought fruit, covered in promise, washed in the blood of Jesus, who died on the Cross to take away our poison. We're the Christians, and He's the Christ. Which means when He looks at the Church, the tree filled with poisoned fruit, He still dares to call us "good."

My pastor dragged me, an angry, bitter sinner, through the valley of the shadow of death to a table set there. There's a cup that runneth over, full of the blood of the risen Lord. It forgives me. It sustains me. He handed me a blood-soaked baton. It changes my song. Surely goodness and mercy shall follow me all the days of my life. I don't need a beach and some footprints. Just a baton and an old cup. Someday it might be yours, too. Run.

Letter 20 – End Times

Rev. Bryan Wolfmueller

Jesus taught clearly and often that He would return in glory to judge the quick and the dead. "'Then the sign of the Son of Man will appear in heaven, and then all the tribes of the earth will mourn, and they will see the Son of Man coming on the clouds of heaven with power and great glory'" (Matthew 24:30 NKJV[1]). "'When the Son of Man comes in His glory, and all the holy angels with Him, then He will sit on the throne of His glory. All the nations will be gathered before Him, and He will separate them one from another'" (Matthew 25:31-32).

The apostles preached the Second Coming. Paul, for example, writes: "For the Lord Himself will descend from heaven with a shout, with the voice of an archangel, and with the trumpet of God. And the dead in Christ will rise first" (1 Thessalonians 4:16). And Peter: "But the day of the Lord will come as a thief in the night, in which the heavens will pass away with a great noise, and the elements will melt with fervent heat; both the earth and the works that are in it will be burned up" (2 Peter 3:10).

The Holy Scriptures end with this promise straight from the mouth of our Lord Jesus: "Surely I am coming quickly!" (Revelation 22:7, 20) What a promise! One day, any day, the Lord Jesus will return to the earth in His glory, will bring up everyone from the dead, will gather together His people into eternal glory, and cast off the workers of iniquity (along with the devil and the demons) into

---

[1] Scriptures in this letter quoted from the New King James Version of the Holy Bible. Emphases added.

eternal death. And we will dwell with the Father, Son, and Holy Spirit in the new heavens and new earth, the home of the righteous. What a glorious hope! No wonder John taught us to pray, "Amen! Come, Lord Jesus!" (Revelation 22:20)

The promise of the return of our Lord Jesus has two major functions in preaching and the life of the Christian: repentance and hope. But these two purposes are confused by the approach most people take to eschatology (the doctrine of last things). If handled poorly, eschatology is distracting or worse, can cause fear and troubled consciences. Your job as a Lutheran pastor is to do better, to prepare the Christian to be ready for Jesus' return. This readiness is both of the Law and the Gospel: repentance and hope.

Your typical evangelical radio preacher approaches the topic of the End Times and Second Coming with the Bible in one hand, and with the newspaper in the other. They treat the promises of the Second Coming and the signs leading up to it as a puzzle to be solved or, better, as a conspiracy to be exposed. "This new technology is the mark of the beast." "This new United Nations chairperson is the antichrist." "Russia is Gog and the Chinese army is preparing for the battle of Armageddon." Some go further and see the reestablishment of Israel as a nation as a fulfillment of Biblical prophecy. They are waiting for the rebuilding of the temple in Jerusalem before the promises of Matthew 24 can be fulfilled.

This was me. When I was 19, I backpacked around Israel so that I could "see biblical prophecy unfold before my eyes." But this is a wrong-headed approach to the Scriptures, and it obscures the true and godly purposes that the Lord would accomplish in us with the Second Coming promises.

We'll note four ways this approach to the Second Coming gets in the way of repentance and hope.

First, the time of the Second Coming is unknown and unknowable. Jesus says, "But of that day and hour no one knows, not even the angels of heaven, but My Father only" (Matthew 24:36). These words should put an end to all speculation and calculation. "It is not for you to know times or seasons which the Father has put in His own authority" (Acts 1:7). Any attempt to discern the timing of the Second Coming is a form of witchcraft, fortunetelling, and is forbidden strictly in the Scriptures. This is not our concern, and any approach to the End Times that encourages this approach is not God-pleasing.

Second, Jesus gives us "not signs." "Take heed that no one deceives you. For many will come in My name, saying, 'I am the Christ,' and will deceive many. And you will hear of wars and rumors of wars. See that you are not troubled; for all these things must come to pass, but *the end is not yet*. For nation will rise against nation, and kingdom against kingdom. And there will be famines, pestilences, and earthquakes in various places. *All these are the beginning of sorrows*" (Matthew 24:4-8, emphasis added).

Notice all the terrible things that are going to be normal: earthquakes, wars, persecution. When we see these things we don't think, "The end is near," but, "This is how it goes in the world and with the Church." Jesus is telling us these things so that we don't get worked up into a frenzy, but instead wait with patience.

Third, we are in it for the long haul. When the Bible tells us about the Second Coming, it prepares us to wait. The Bridegroom was delayed and the ten virgins fell asleep (Matthew 25:5) and the owner of the vineyard went to a far country for a long time (Luke 20:9). Peter speaks most clearly of the need for patience while we wait for the Lord's return: ". . . scoffers will come in the last days, walking according to their own lusts, and saying, 'Where is the promise of His coming? For since the fathers fell asleep, all things continue as they were from the beginning of creation.' But, beloved, do not forget this one thing, that with the Lord one day is as a thousand years, and a thousand years as one day. The Lord is not slack concerning His promise, as some count slackness, but is longsuffering toward us, not willing that any should perish but that all should come to repentance" (2 Peter 3:3-4, 8-9).

Fourth, while we are ready to wait with patience and endure hardship, we also live in great expectancy. "For yet a little while, and He who is coming will come and will not tarry" (Hebrews 10:37, quoting Habakkuk 2:3). Jesus could return at any moment. We call this truth the *imminent* return of Christ. "The Lord is at hand" (Philippians 4:5). This means (and let this sink in) there are no prophecies that need to be fulfilled before the Lord returns. Nothing needs to happen in Israel before the Lord comes in glory. At any moment (and this has been true for centuries) the trumpet could sound, and

the archangel shout, and the sky rend, and the Lord Jesus appear on
the clouds as on a throne.

The preaching of the Second Coming is a preaching of watchfulness, but this is what we are watching for: the glory of Jesus.

- *"Watch therefore*, for you do not know what hour your Lord is
  coming'" (Matthew 24:42).
- "'Therefore you also *be ready*, for the Son of Man is coming at an
  hour you do not expect'" (Luke 12:40).
- *"Watch therefore*, and pray always that you may be counted worthy
  to escape all these things that will come to pass, and to stand before
  the Son of Man'" (Luke 21:36).
- "... *looking for* the blessed hope and glorious appearing of our great
  God and Savior Jesus Christ" (Titus 2:13).
- "But the end of all things is at hand; therefore *be serious and watch-
  ful* in your prayers" (1 Peter 4:7).
- "... *looking for and hastening* the coming of the day of God"
  (2 Peter 3:12).

While it is good to discern the times and understand our place
in history, the Christian focus is on being ready for Jesus' return. This
readiness is both of the Law and the Gospel. The readiness of the Law
is repentance and its fruit: good works.

Jesus warns the church in Ephesus, "'Remember therefore from
where you have fallen; repent and do the first works, or else I will come
to you quickly and remove your lampstand from its place—unless you
repent'" (Revelation 2:5). We know we are sinners who have broken
God's commands and offended His holiness. This, though, is the
work of Jesus on the Cross, atoning for sinners, suffering in our place.
We despise our sin and trust His mercy, and He is faithful and just
to forgive our sins and cleanse us from all unrighteousness. Because
of the suffering of Jesus there is nothing to fear on Judgment Day.
"There is therefore now no condemnation to those who are in Christ
Jesus" (Romans 8:1).

And good works follow repentance. Consider the Parable of the
Talents (Luke 19:11-27). Jesus has entrusted us with Gifts and offices,
and by the strength of the Holy Spirit we serve our neighbors. Our
watchfulness is a diligent, sober, prayerful watching, a stewardship
of time the Lord gives us before it is all rolled up as a scroll.

The readiness of the Gospel is hope. The Last Day is not fearful for the Christian. It is Jesus, the One who died for you, the One who loves you, who is coming back. He returns with hands raised in blessing, the same hands pierced for you. The return of Jesus is, for you, a rescue mission. He comes to take us from this valley of sorrow and death to the glory of the resurrection and the bliss of seeing Him face to face.

His return, then, is not intimidating or frightful, but the thing we long for and need the most. Here's how Jesus puts it: "'Now when these things begin to happen, look up and lift up your heads, because your redemption draws near'" (Luke 21:28).

On the Last Day our Redeemer, our Savior, our Friend, our Substitute, our King, our Jesus draws near. God be praised! Amen! Come, Lord Jesus! Amen.

Letter 21 – Law and Gospel

Rev. Seth Clemmer

When our Lord speaks, He's not just *talking about things*—He's *doing* something to those who hear. The Word of God is living and active (Hebrews 4:12), bringing repentance and working faith as He pleases—so when Jesus speaks, He is working on those who hear. He sends His Word through His prophets, apostles, pastors, Christians, etc., and through it, accomplishes what He wants it to do (Isaiah 55:11).

This is helpful to keep in mind as we consider subjects such as "the distinction between Law and Gospel" in our Lord's Word. You and I might study the ideas of "God's Law" and "God's Gospel" but they are not abstract ideas—they are the active Word of God. Our Lord does not deal in abstractions; He deals with us concretely.

But what's He doing?

Our Lord has His Word of Law spoken to sinners to give us the Gift of repentance, that our Old Adam, our sinful flesh, would be killed and turned from our idols and evil ways, and that a new man, the man of faith, would be made holy, given life, and set free to love and serve others.

This is demonstrated beautifully when a rich man approached Jesus and asked, "Good Teacher, what must I do to inherit eternal life?" (Mark 10:17-22)

As we consider that conversation, we must keep in mind that Jesus is not interested in simply answering a question about theology and how one is to be saved. If that were the case, He might have said something like, "Well, you can't be saved by anything *you* do, obviously, but only by grace!" End of conversation—point made. But Jesus wasn't simply teaching about theology, He was *doing something* to the man and to us who hear His Word today.

Jesus wanted to tear something out of the rich man's grip: his idol. Surprisingly, Jesus answered the man by telling him to keep the commandments: "You know the commandments: 'Do not murder, Do not commit adultery, Do not steal, Do not bear false witness, Do not defraud, Honor your father and mother.'" Really? Keep the Law? The rich man, and all of fallen humanity, had the Law already before Jesus came. He didn't need to hear Jesus say that just for information, but that was never Jesus' goal. Jesus wanted to *do something* to the man: repent him.

In response to Jesus, the rich man said, "Teacher, all these I have kept from my youth." Now, you and I know that no one keeps the Law perfectly, especially since the Law must be kept in the heart and not only outwardly (Matthew 5:21-22, 27-28). But again, Jesus isn't just answering a question; He's doing something. "And Jesus, looking at him, loved him, and said to him, 'You lack one thing: go, sell all that you have and give to the poor, and you will have treasure in heaven; and come, follow me'" (Mark 10:21).

"Sell everything, give it away, and follow me," said Jesus. As much as it might have seemed like it, Jesus wasn't giving the rich man something more to do, as though Jesus was giving him a way of salvation apart from the Cross. Jesus wasn't saying, "You don't need me to die for you—you just need to sell everything and follow me." After all, Jesus didn't come to give us more laws or alternate paths to the Father. Instead, He came to die for sinners. So, in this conversation, Jesus was *doing* something to the rich man. He was showing that this man's wealth had become his god. "Disheartened by the saying, he went away sorrowful, for he had great possessions." Having exposed his idol, the Law had done its job.

God's Word isn't just *about* things, but it *does something* to those who hear. Jesus had smashed this man's idol and devastated any hope he had of being righteous on his own merits. And that's right where Jesus wanted him—totally dependent upon His mercy. Sinners, like the rich man and us, are quick to think that we're good at keeping the Law, quick to point out the sins of one another, and slow to see how entangled we are in our own idols. Sinners, like the rich man and us, need to be shown that they are sinners so that they rejoice in the life-giving Gospel. So Jesus takes His Law and shines a light on our idols.

In the case of the rich man, the Law shined a light on his wealth. What is it that you hold onto and depend upon as though you couldn't imagine life without it? Jesus wants to rip out of your grip those idols you're refusing to turn from. It may be wealth or the lack of it; it may be your coveting the life or possessions or spouse of others. It may be your desire to judge others with the Law instead of yourself; it may be your being stingy and selfish instead of encouraging and helping others with generosity. It may be your pride and desire to always have control over things around you. It may be your earthly success and social status that you hold onto most tightly. It may be something else—we all have different idols to which we cling.

Jesus wants to tear them from your grip and give you the one thing that matters: Himself.

His brutal Law exposes those things we really don't want to let go. It's a harsh Law, to be sure, but it's still a Word of love from a merciful Lord. After all, if He didn't love us, why would He bother speaking His Law and turning us from those idols that cannot save, cannot help, cannot comfort, and can only harm us?

Jesus speaks the Law in love. Notice that just before Jesus smashes him with the Law, Mark specifically says that Jesus looked at the man and *loved* him: "And Jesus, looking at him, *loved* him, and said to him, 'You lack one thing...'" It was in love that Jesus had to bring the hammer of the Law, for to let the man cling to his idol was no love at all. He had to rip out the thing doing the damage—the idol in which the man was trusting instead of Jesus alone.

In love for you, your Lord uses His Law to show you what your false gods are and to tear them out of your grip. He then freely places in your hands His own righteousness—that which you were never able to earn or deserve. He gives you His full wealth of salvation—not silver and gold, but His holy precious blood and innocent suffering and death by which He bought you. Having used His Law to rip from you any hope of making yourself worthy, He gives you all that He gained on the Cross.

Your Lord knows the things you don't quite want to release from your grip: the lust that brings you its empty promises, the hatred you keep trying to justify against your neighbor, the longing for just a little bit more, the desire to be liked by others no matter what it takes...

Your Lord wants to set you free. He doesn't simply want to tell you *about* Law and Gospel, but He wants to *do something* to you. So, He does. He has His Word of Law spoken to you, turning you from sin and working the Gift of repentance. He has His Word of Gospel spoken to you, bringing life and forgiveness, covering shame, removing guilt, and strengthening you in love toward others. Jesus does it all. He tears the idols out of *your* hands and grips you tightly with *His* nail-scarred hands—for you belong to Him.

Through the Office of the Holy Ministry, the Lord has that Word of Law and Gospel spoken to sinners. We, the Lord's pastors, don't merely talk *about* theology to those whom we shepherd, but Jesus *does something* to those who hear, when and where He pleases. To be sure, it is a daunting task to faithfully administer His Word in preaching, teaching, and pastoral care. Yet, it is a joyful and rewarding task as sinners are freed from the haunting voices of sin and devil and are turned to the merciful voice of their Lord Jesus.

Letter 22 – Fraternity of the Pastor

Rev. Timothy Appel

"Am I my brother's keeper?" (Genesis 4:9) You know the answer to Cain's infamous question. Yes, you are your brother's keeper. But then there's the infamous question from the lawyer (Luke 10:29), rephrased ever so slightly: "And who is my brother?"

God's Holy Word answers this question in several ways. Most broadly, each and every human being is a brother. Each and every human being has been created in the image of God (Genesis 9:6); each and every human being traces his lineage back to Adam (Acts 17:26). Therefore, every person you encounter is a brother whom God has given you to love according to your various vocations.

More specifically, each and every Christian is a brother. The Son of God shares our humanity in His Incarnation (Hebrews 2:17); by virtue of His death and resurrection for sinners, He has made His disciples His brothers (John 20:17). Therefore, every Christian you encounter is a brother to whom you are bound in deepest love and closest fellowship (1 John 1:7; 2:10).

Even more specifically, each and every man whom the Lord calls to serve in His Office of the Holy Ministry is a brother. Those who share in Christ's call to preach His Word and administer His Sacraments (1 Corinthians 4:1) are bound together in a unique service to the Lord and His Church (Acts 6:2). Therefore, pastors are brothers in the Lord, united in His divine call as servants of the Gospel.

This final brotherhood is our primary consideration here. As one who desires the noble task of being a pastor in Christ's Church (1 Timothy 3:1), what does it mean for you to be your brother's keeper? What does it mean for pastors who share the evangelical Lutheran confession of the faith to care for each other as brothers?

Again, God's Holy Word answers this question in several ways. King Solomon writes in Proverbs 27:17, "Iron sharpens iron, and one man sharpens another." Your time at seminary is a great blessing from the Lord. There, He forms you to serve as a pastor in His Church. He places you at the feet of wise and faithful professors. He places you side-by-side with eager and diligent classmates. He fills your heart with His Word through rigorous academic classes and daily devotional life in chapel. In this way, the Lord forms you for service in His Church.

But the Lord does not stop doing this once you graduate from seminary. The Lord keeps forming you for service in His Church through "the mutual conversation and consolation of the brethren" (*Smalcald Articles*, Part III, Article IV). When you engage with your brother pastors in the Word of God, you sharpen each other in your own Christian faith and in your service to your individual parishes. One pastor brings his knowledge of Hebrew and Greek to uncover exegetical insight. Another shares his wisdom gained from years of experience of shepherding the flock. Yet another adds his ability to explain a large amount of material succinctly and faithfully. As pastors together pick up the sharp, two-edged sword of the living and active Word of God (Hebrews 4:12), each brother sharpens the other.

King Solomon also writes in Ecclesiastes 4:9-12, "Two are better than one, because they have a good reward for their toil. For if they fall, one will lift up his fellow. But woe to him who is alone when he falls and has not another to lift him up! Again, if two lie together, they keep warm, but how can one keep warm alone? And though a man might prevail against one who is alone, two will withstand him—a threefold cord is not quickly broken." The Lord Jesus can and does work through one man for the sake of many; consider the faithfulness of Daniel in the face of a pit full of lions. Yet the Lord has placed each one among the whole Body of Christ in order to strengthen their common confession of the truth; remember how Shadrach, Meshach, and Abednego stood together in the face of a fiery furnace.

So it is for the brotherhood of pastors. The Lord works through the sole pastor in the small rural parish to bring the fullness of His Gifts to even two or three gathered in His Name (Matthew 18:20). Yet the Lord also places multiple pastors in one parish to stand together in common confession of the Christian faith. He places multiple pastors into one circuit to work together for the sake of His entire Church on earth. You do not work in the Lord's vineyard alone; He places other pastors right there with you to support you and strengthen you, not only for the sake of His work in your community, but for the sake of His Gospel going to the ends of the earth (Acts 1:8).

Jesus speaks in Matthew 18:15, "If your brother sins against you, go and tell him his fault, between you and him alone. If he listens to you, you have gained your brother." Perhaps it seems unimaginable that brothers in the ministerium of the Lutheran Church-Missouri Synod would sin against each other, but trust me, it happens. This sin, however, does not end the love that one brother owes the other. The brother goes to his erring brother. A pastor who ignores the false teaching of his brother pastor is not showing love. A pastor who turns a blind eye to the persistent sinful life of another pastor is not being his brother's keeper. To let the wolf attack and kill one of the Lord's under-shepherds without warning that brother is to act as the hired hand who cares only for his own skin (John 10:12-13). Instead, you love your brother pastor by calling him to repentance, when needed, and helping him to see his blind spots. Of course, that can only be done when the plank has been removed from your own eye first (Matthew 7:5). Part of living as a brother pastor is the wise and willing acceptance of correction and rebuke when you are the one who needs it (Proverbs 17:10).

Paul writes in Galatians 6:2, "Bear one another's burdens, and so fulfill the law of Christ." The Lord did not intend for you to serve in the Office of the Holy Ministry all alone. You won't make it very far if you try. He has placed your brother pastors beside you to help you bear your burdens. He has given them to comfort you with the Gospel when despair is knocking at your door. He has given them to pray for you and with you when congregational and family difficulties trouble you. He has given them to give you counsel in the Holy Scriptures and *Lutheran Confessions* when you aren't sure what you should say or do next. He has given them to point you always away from your sufficiency and only toward the sufficiency of Christ (2 Corinthians 3:5). He has given you the same to do for them in their time of need.

Paul tells the Ephesian pastors in Acts 20:28, "Pay careful attention to yourselves and to all the flock, in which the Holy Spirit has made you overseers, to care for the church of God, which he obtained with his own blood." Complacency has no place in the Office of the Holy Ministry. Pastors are called to pay attention to themselves. That is true for the individual pastor paying attention to his own doctrine, life, and practice; that is true for pastors paying attention to each other. The Office of the Holy Ministry requires careful attention.

Certainly, such careful attention is needed among brother pastors so that the Word of God is taught in its truth and purity in the Church and so that pastors lead their congregations by example of holy life according to God's Word (*Small Catechism*, First Petition of the Lord's Prayer). Yet, such careful attention is also needed among brother pastors so that these men, who are themselves members of God's flock, receive spiritual care in their time of need. Pastors regularly make hospital visits for their own parishioners; who goes to see the pastor when he is in the hospital? Pastors regularly pray with members in their most dire moments; who prays with the pastor when his road is dark? It is quite true that God has given the Church to care for His pastors (Galatians 6:6), yet brother pastors also ought to pay attention to each other here. Watch out for your brother pastor in his time of need and serve him with the Gospel of God.

In these ways, pastors are blessed to live the reality for which King David prays in Psalm 133:1, "Behold, how good and pleasant it is when brothers dwell in unity!" You are your brother's keeper, and he is yours. Take up the task joyfully, knowing that your Brother Jesus Christ keeps you, all His pastors, and His entire Church on earth in the true faith unto life everlasting.

Letter 23 – On Being a Missionary

By Rev. Roy S. Askins

So, you are interested in serving as a foreign missionary. Living in a foreign culture and serving them with the Gospel is no minor task; it will challenge your heart and mind. It requires an unswerving dedication to God and His Word, as well as to immersing yourself in Lutheran doctrine, and distinguishing Law and Gospel.

The Lord provides many opportunities for service in His kingdom. Serving as a missionary requires special study and preparation, not because the work is inherently different, but because it should not be approached inappropriately, namely, as an opportunity to travel and see the world. While short-term missions can be helpful, they can create a tourist mentality; you go and work, all the while knowing that you will be home in a few weeks. Anyone can endure hardship for a few weeks. A long-term missionary serves indefinitely, which requires an entirely different mindset for him and his family.

How do you prepare to serve as a missionary? Let's use the analogy of packing for a trip. You can certainly find numerous guides on how to pack; just search YouTube. That is the "easy" part. Perhaps more difficult to find, yet vastly more important, is advice for packing your mind. What should you prepare for mentally as you consider the work of a missionary? What mental baggage, in a good sense, should you bring?

God's Word in Excess

When packing for international travel, YouTubers typically advise their viewers to pack light. Too much baggage means you will spend more time managing your luggage and less time enjoying the trip. As a missionary, however, you should do the opposite. Pack your knowledge of God's Word in excess.

Know God's Word inside and out. Missionaries must be ready to give an answer for the hope that they have (1 Peter 3:15) at a moment's notice. A missionary needs the Word of God written on his heart and mind, not simply in a book or on a smartphone. In other words, memorize God's Word. Pack it in excess.

This also means knowing Greek and Hebrew. When you can parse your Greek and Hebrew, you can feast on the marrow of God's Word, delving deeply into its context and meaning both in the original context and today. Learning the Word of God in Greek and Hebrew will help place you into the mind of God's people, into the "mind" of the Scripture. Knowing Greek and Hebrew will also help you translate the "mind" of Scripture into the language and culture of the people to whom God has sent you to preach and proclaim.

Learning the original languages of the Bible will also help you prepare to live in another culture. After all, the most important part of living in another culture is learning the language. Beyond simply being able to communicate with them, the language will give you insight into the thought and culture of the people that speak that language. In this way you clear the way for the Gospel to be understood within their patterns.

Consider this example: You cannot understand Chinese culture apart from an understanding of family relationships. This becomes abundantly clear when you learn the Chinese vocabulary for family members. They do not simply have "sister" or "brother," but specific words for "oldest brother" and "youngest sister." When your siblings refer to you as "brother," it reinforces your place in the family. You are not merely a brother, but you are the youngest brother. This terminology also includes extended family. Your title places you within the family and therefore also dictates your responsibilities and place in life. So we clearly see in this example how the culture and language work in tandem: You cannot fully understand the importance of family in Chinese culture until you also learn the Chinese language.

Lutheran Confessions in Abundance

Next, pack the fundamentals of Lutheran theology, namely, the *Lutheran Confessions*. There is a common misconception that they have no place on the mission field. Rather, many Christians think that "mere Christianity" or simply the "basics of the faith" shared by all Christian denominations is all that is necessary. This false misconception above grows out of the belief that all Christians essentially believe the same thing, that teaching distinctively Lutheran theology will merely introduce the theological battles of the Western Church into a "pure," or "new," church. We need to expunge such false thinking from our midst, for it does not grow out of the certainty found in the *Book of Concord*.

Specifically, this perspective fails on multiple accounts, but here are two major issues. First, the teachings of the Lutheran Church are not simply "Lutheran" but are the teachings of the *Una Sancta*, the one Holy Christian Church of all space and time. We do not preach Lutheran doctrine and confess Lutheran dogma because we merely prefer that type of theology or because we think Martin Luther was some type of patron saint. We hold to Lutheran doctrine because it is, first and foremost, evangelical in the classic sense of the term. Through Luther, Christ brought to light again the teaching of the *evangel*—the Gospel—out of the false doctrine and teachings of Roman Catholicism. The teachings of this evangelical—Lutheran—faith are the teachings of Scripture. When we take Lutheran doctrine to the mission field, therefore, we are not taking the teachings of simply one denomination over and against another, but we preach the very Word of God, purely and correctly. We are not, in this sense, preaching the Lutheran faith, but the biblical faith.

Secondly, the Church has spent the last 2000 years working out Christian doctrine, struggling over words and confessions, weeding out heresy and false teaching, seeking to preserve the unity of the Spirit in the bond of peace. Is it loving to force new church bodies to struggle anew? Why would we not include them in the last 2000 years of conversation so that they also might benefit from the work of faithful Christians and theologians who have come before us? It is an unloving father indeed who refuses to pass to his sons the years of accumulated wisdom so that they might avoid some of his errors and walk a better path than he did.

Law and Gospel Aplenty

Pack your mind with thorough knowledge of C.F.W. Walther's book, *Law & Gospel: How to Read and Apply the Bible.* The subtitle says it all. The proper distinction between the Law and the Gospel provides the framework for providing the cure and care of souls in your home context and abroad.

During my service in Asia, I interviewed a missionary who was teaching pastoral care in the Philippines. I asked him how teaching in the Philippines differed from teaching and applying pastoral care in the USA. His answer gets to the heart of our discussion here. He pointed out that regardless of country, language, or age, sinners are sinners. They are turned inward, focused on their own desires. The pastor and missionary must apply Law and Gospel to the sinner in the foreign context just as much as the pastor applies Law and Gospel at home. Foreign or domestic, our fundamental connection to God's Word takes place within the structure of Law and Gospel. You must ask yourself, does this text condemn the sinner or does this text bind up his wounds, forgiving his sins, and point him to Christ, his Savior?

This means the fundamental connection between the Word of God and whatever culture you live within takes place within this same framework: Law and Gospel. Sinners are sinners whether they live in Texas or Vietnam. All must be convicted of their sin, and all must be healed and forgiven in the proclamation of the Gospel.

Take the Journey

Pack your mental baggage and pack it well. Service as a missionary is not easy and not for the faint of heart. It requires a deep and abiding knowledge of God's Word and Lutheran doctrine, as well as knowledge of how to apply God's Word in Law and Gospel. If you "have a heart for missions" but do not have this baggage packed yet, then go and gain this baggage first. Take courses at one of the LCMS Concordia universities or at one of the two seminaries. Consider earning a master's degree and being deployed as a pastor. The journey will be hard, but, having properly packed, you will be better prepared to give an answer for the hope that is in you.

Letter 24 – On Being Lutheran

Rev. Dr. Erik Herrmann

I've been told you've been starting to wonder about what it means to be a Lutheran. Perhaps you have completed studying Luther's *Small Catechism* and have been "confirmed" (a strange word that we will have to skip discussing here). Perhaps you have had a conversation with friends who aren't Lutheran but are Baptist, or Roman Catholic, or United Church of Christ, or Presbyterian, or non-denominational, or nothing really at all … and they asked you, "What's a Lutheran?" and you felt a little tongue-tied. Or perhaps it is a passing thought on your way to not caring about what it means to be Lutheran, because, after all, does it really matter and aren't all churches basically the same?

Of course, maybe the thought has occurred to you that being Lutheran is simply an accident of where you are born or who your family is. If you were born in a country that is 90% Muslim, would you have been a Lutheran? Probably not. But that doesn't really say much about what it means to be Lutheran or whether it is true. If Sir Isaac Newton were not born in England but rather in China, and instead of sitting under a ripe apple tree in Cambridge, he sat under a Flying Spider Monkey tree fern … then the apple would not have fallen onto his head and he would have never scribbled down the theory of gravity. But so what? There would still be gravity. The truth of gravity is true whether one has a theory for it or not … whether one believes in it or not. So, part of the question of what it means to be Lutheran is a question of truth. Are the things that Lutherans talk about, pray about, love, and hope for … are they true? Are they real like gravity or are they just a product of culture, or perspective, or preference?

But first we should point out that "Lutheran" is actually an unfriendly nickname, given by the critics and opponents of those who thought Martin Luther wasn't worth listening to when he talked about Jesus. Luther himself didn't like it and preferred simply "Christian." (Luther: "Why should the children of Christ call themselves by my wretched name?") His friends often used the name "evangelical," which just means "Gospel people," and that gets quite a bit closer to it. Because, in the end, it's not the name that matters but what we believe. And what we believe is the Gospel.

Lutherans are obsessed with the Gospel, laser-focused on it. Among all Christians, in all places, we find that it is our calling to confess the Gospel. We know that the Gospel isn't the whole song (there is creation and the Law, and beauty and good works, and the mystery of black holes and mathematics and video games, as well as cancer and jazz and peer pressure and politics and pandemics), but we believe it is the best part of the song—the song's main theme and main chorus, and that without it, the song would not be very good at all.

But the Gospel is more than a theme or a chorus. It's more than some lovely ideas about God or a story about Jesus. It's more than even the fancy church-word, "doctrine." The Gospel is something real … the really Real Presence of God in this world, in His Son, in His Son's words because His Son is the Word, the Word made flesh who dwells among us (John 1:14).

The Gospel is the Good News that God has not abandoned the world—even though it seems like the world is spinning out of control. Though it may be hard to believe, what with hurricanes and earthquakes, and people without enough food or clean water, and senseless suffering and war; nevertheless, God is here. He has always been here even though we have thought to build towers to reach Him or launch rockets into the heavens to make a name for ourselves. God is here and He is close, as Paul said to the Athenians, "He is actually not far from each one of us for, 'In Him we live and move and have our being'" (Acts 17:27f). And not only is He present in this world, but the Gospel is the glad tidings that He loves this world, loves us in this world, even though we have made an enormous mess of this world and ourselves. And that love has been made known in Jesus Christ, God's Son.

The Gospel is the declaration that God's love for us is more profound and reckless than any love we can imagine. Not for good folks, got-their-lives-together folks, or better-than-most folks, but for us sinners Christ died. For us sinners He suffers, He forgives, He delivers from death, promising us life by the strength of His resurrection from the dead.

And even more than this (can there really be more than this?) the Gospel is the promise that Christ has chosen to come and meet us today in His Word—those written words of poets and prophets and apostles that we call the Bible, those words proclaimed from the pulpit by the pastor, the words that accompany water and bread and wine. Christ is here. In our joy and our sorrow He has joined Himself to us, like the vows of a wedding—"for better or worse, in sickness and in health, to love and to cherish"—yet without the "until death do we part!"

From this obsession with the Gospel, Lutherans conclude a variety of things about how to live in this world. We don't have space in this letter to list and explain all of them but we can sum it up in its most important and overarching theme: FREEDOM. It's actually kind of in our (nick)name. Martin Luther's last name sounds a lot like the Greek word for "free" (eLeUTHERios), and so, when he discovered this Gospel he started signing his name like that: Martin Eleutherius—Martin the Free One.

Now in America there is a lot of talk about freedom—political freedom, religious freedom. But the freedom of the Gospel is really something quite different. "For freedom Christ has set us free!" said the apostle Paul (Galatians 5:1). But he does not mean freedom as in independence, freedom to do or take whatever we want. Paul means freedom from prison, a prison that is in many ways a prison of our own making. Sin is this prison because it ties down our thoughts and actions only towards ourselves. We put ourselves in the center of the universe, thinking this will make us happy, but instead we are forever stuck, trying to figure out how to make our lives better or at least appear better before others. Like constantly tweaking an Instagram pic with filters and Photoshop, we are continually worried about how we look (yes, physically, but also in every other way—successful, smart, interesting, etc.). Even if we don't care about others, we are obsessed with wanting others to care about us. We judge others, but we don't want others to judge us. And we certainly don't want God to judge us.

But now, because of Christ, because of His forgiveness, we have freedom from all the ways that our sin holds us captive. We have freedom from the Law of God that judges and condemns us, freedom from the accusations it makes against us because of our sins. But we also have freedom for God's Law—to love and delight in the beautiful life it describes even though it is a life that the Law cannot give. We now have freedom to receive, without embarrassment or hesitation, absolutely everything from the hand of God. Freedom to love without strings attached, without trying to get something out of it, without trying to earn God's favor or the favor of others. Freedom from grief without hope, freedom from the petrifying fear of death, freedom to suffer for others without need of reward, recognition, or payback. Freedom to simply be a beloved child of God, knowing that whatever happens this will never change. "For I am sure that neither death nor life, nor angels nor rulers, nor things present nor things to come, nor powers, nor height nor depth, nor anything else in all creation, will be able to separate us from the love of God in Christ Jesus our Lord" (Romans 8:38-39).

So that's it for now. I hope you noticed how I did *not* answer the question. Being Lutheran is not being German or Swedish or Norwegian, going to potlucks, eating brats or lutefisk or lefse. It's not even singing your favorite hymns or carols. To be Lutheran is to be free ... free in all the ways that really matter ... free to be a child of God, free to love your neighbor, free to be Christ's own, "to live under Him in His kingdom and serve Him in everlasting righteousness, innocence, and blessedness, just as He is risen from the dead, lives and reigns to all eternity. This is most certainly true."

Higher Things would like to acknowledge and thank **LCMS** *Set Apart to Serve* for their contributions in making this project a reality.

Learn more about **LCMS** *Set Apart to Serve* at https://www.lcms.org/set-apart-to-serve

Printed in the USA
CPSIA information can be obtained
at www.ICGtesting.com
JSHW021537080823
46155JS00003B/10

9 781956 658323